CS-9   GENERAL APTITUDE AND ABILITIES SERIES

This is your
PASSBOOK for...

Civil Service Spelling

Test Preparation Study Guide
Questions & Answers

COPYRIGHT NOTICE

This book is SOLELY intended for, is sold ONLY to, and its use is RESTRICTED to individual, bona fide applicants or candidates who qualify by virtue of having seriously filed applications for appropriate license, certificate, professional and/or promotional advancement, higher school matriculation, scholarship, or other legitimate requirements of education and/or governmental authorities.

This book is NOT intended for use, class instruction, tutoring, training, duplication, copying, reprinting, excerption, or adaptation, etc., by:

1) Other publishers
2) Proprietors and/or Instructors of "Coaching" and/or Preparatory Courses
3) Personnel and/or Training Divisions of commercial, industrial, and governmental organizations
4) Schools, colleges, or universities and/or their departments and staffs, including teachers and other personnel
5) Testing Agencies or Bureaus
6) Study groups which seek by the purchase of a single volume to copy and/or duplicate and/or adapt this material for use by the group as a whole without having purchased individual volumes for each of the members of the group
7) Et al.

Such persons would be in violation of appropriate Federal and State statutes.

PROVISION OF LICENSING AGREEMENTS – Recognized educational, commercial, industrial, and governmental institutions and organizations, and others legitimately engaged in educational pursuits, including training, testing, and measurement activities, may address request for a licensing agreement to the copyright owners, who will determine whether, and under what conditions, including fees and charges, the materials in this book may be used them. In other words, a licensing facility exists for the legitimate use of the material in this book on other than an individual basis. However, it is asseverated and affirmed here that the material in this book CANNOT be used without the receipt of the express permission of such a licensing agreement from the Publishers. Inquiries re licensing should be addressed to the company, attention rights and permissions department.

All rights reserved, including the right of reproduction in whole or in part, in any form or by any means, electronic or mechanical, including photocopying, recording, or by any information storage and retrieval system, without permission in writing from the Publisher.

Copyright © 2024 by
National Learning Corporation

212 Michael Drive, Syosset, NY 11791
(516) 921-8888 • www.passbooks.com
E-mail: info@passbooks.com

PUBLISHED IN THE UNITED STATES OF AMERICA

PASSBOOK® SERIES

THE *PASSBOOK® SERIES* has been created to prepare applicants and candidates for the ultimate academic battlefield – the examination room.

At some time in our lives, each and every one of us may be required to take an examination – for validation, matriculation, admission, qualification, registration, certification, or licensure.

Based on the assumption that every applicant or candidate has met the basic formal educational standards, has taken the required number of courses, and read the necessary texts, the *PASSBOOK® SERIES* furnishes the one special preparation which may assure passing with confidence, instead of failing with insecurity. Examination questions – together with answers – are furnished as the basic vehicle for study so that the mysteries of the examination and its compounding difficulties may be eliminated or diminished by a sure method.

This book is meant to help you pass your examination provided that you qualify and are serious in your objective.

The entire field is reviewed through the huge store of content information which is succinctly presented through a provocative and challenging approach – the question-and-answer method.

A climate of success is established by furnishing the correct answers at the end of each test.

You soon learn to recognize types of questions, forms of questions, and patterns of questioning. You may even begin to anticipate expected outcomes.

You perceive that many questions are repeated or adapted so that you can gain acute insights, which may enable you to score many sure points.

You learn how to confront new questions, or types of questions, and to attack them confidently and work out the correct answers.

You note objectives and emphases, and recognize pitfalls and dangers, so that you may make positive educational adjustments.

Moreover, you are kept fully informed in relation to new concepts, methods, practices, and directions in the field.

You discover that you are actually taking the examination all the time: you are preparing for the examination by "taking" an examination, not by reading extraneous and/or supererogatory textbooks.

In short, this PASSBOOK®, used directedly, should be an important factor in helping you to pass your test.

CIVIL SERVICE SPELLING

The General Aptitude and Abilities Series provides functional, intensive test practice and drill in the basic skills and areas common to many civil service, general aptitude and achievement examinations necessary for entrance into schools or occupations.

Passbooks in this series use a variety of question types, and other applicable items like charts, graphs, illustrations and more, to prepare candidates for testing in particular subject areas. This Passbook features a wide range of questions covering spelling; and more.

HOW TO TAKE A TEST

You have studied long, hard and conscientiously.

With your official admission card in hand, and your heart pounding, you have been admitted to the examination room.

You note that there are several hundred other applicants in the examination room waiting to take the same test.

They all appear to be equally well prepared.

You know that nothing but your best effort will suffice. The "moment of truth" is at hand: you now have to demonstrate objectively, in writing, your knowledge of content and your understanding of subject matter.

You are fighting the most important battle of your life—to pass and/or score high on an examination which will determine your career and provide the economic basis for your livelihood.

What extra, special things should you know and should you do in taking the examination?

I. YOU MUST PASS AN EXAMINATION

A. WHAT EVERY CANDIDATE SHOULD KNOW
Examination applicants often ask us for help in preparing for the written test. What can I study in advance? What kinds of questions will be asked? How will the test be given? How will the papers be graded?

B. HOW ARE EXAMS DEVELOPED?
Examinations are carefully written by trained technicians who are specialists in the field known as "psychological measurement," in consultation with recognized authorities in the field of work that the test will cover. These experts recommend the subject matter areas or skills to be tested; only those knowledges or skills important to your success on the job are included. The most reliable books and source materials available are used as references. Together, the experts and technicians judge the difficulty level of the questions.
Test technicians know how to phrase questions so that the problem is clearly stated. Their ethics do not permit "trick" or "catch" questions. Questions may have been tried out on sample groups, or subjected to statistical analysis, to determine their usefulness.
Written tests are often used in combination with performance tests, ratings of training and experience, and oral interviews. All of these measures combine to form the best-known means of finding the right person for the right job.

II. HOW TO PASS THE WRITTEN TEST

A. BASIC STEPS

1) Study the announcement

How, then, can you know what subjects to study? Our best answer is: "Learn as much as possible about the class of positions for which you've applied." The exam will test the knowledge, skills and abilities needed to do the work.

Your most valuable source of information about the position you want is the official exam announcement. This announcement lists the training and experience qualifications. Check these standards and apply only if you come reasonably close to meeting them. Many jurisdictions preview the written test in the exam announcement by including a section called "Knowledge and Abilities Required," "Scope of the Examination," or some similar heading. Here you will find out specifically what fields will be tested.

2) Choose appropriate study materials

If the position for which you are applying is technical or advanced, you will read more advanced, specialized material. If you are already familiar with the basic principles of your field, elementary textbooks would waste your time. Concentrate on advanced textbooks and technical periodicals. Think through the concepts and review difficult problems in your field.

These are all general sources. You can get more ideas on your own initiative, following these leads. For example, training manuals and publications of the government agency which employs workers in your field can be useful, particularly for technical and professional positions. A letter or visit to the government department involved may result in more specific study suggestions, and certainly will provide you with a more definite idea of the exact nature of the position you are seeking.

3) Study this book!

III. KINDS OF TESTS

Tests are used for purposes other than measuring knowledge and ability to perform specified duties. For some positions, it is equally important to test ability to make adjustments to new situations or to profit from training. In others, basic mental abilities not dependent on information are essential. Questions which test these things may not appear as pertinent to the duties of the position as those which test for knowledge and information. Yet they are often highly important parts of a fair examination. For very general questions, it is almost impossible to help you direct your study efforts. What we can do is to point out some of the more common of these general abilities needed in public service positions and describe some typical questions.

1) General information

Broad, general information has been found useful for predicting job success in some kinds of work. This is tested in a variety of ways, from vocabulary lists to questions about current events. Basic background in some field of work, such as sociology or economics, may be sampled in a group of questions. Often these are principles which have become familiar to most persons through exposure rather than through formal training. It is difficult to advise you how to study for these questions; being alert to the world around you is our best suggestion.

2) Verbal ability

An example of an ability needed in many positions is verbal or language ability. Verbal ability is, in brief, the ability to use and understand words. Vocabulary and grammar tests are typical measures of this ability. Reading comprehension or paragraph interpretation questions are common in many kinds of civil service tests. You are given a paragraph of written material and asked to find its central meaning.

IV. KINDS OF QUESTIONS

1. Multiple-choice Questions

Most popular of the short-answer questions is the "multiple choice" or "best answer" question. It can be used, for example, to test for factual knowledge, ability to solve problems or judgment in meeting situations found at work.

A multiple-choice question is normally one of three types:
- It can begin with an incomplete statement followed by several possible endings. You are to find the one ending which best completes the statement, although some of the others may not be entirely wrong.
- It can also be a complete statement in the form of a question which is answered by choosing one of the statements listed.
- It can be in the form of a problem – again you select the best answer.

Here is an example of a multiple-choice question with a discussion which should give you some clues as to the method for choosing the right answer:

When an employee has a complaint about his assignment, the action which will best help him overcome his difficulty is to
- A. discuss his difficulty with his coworkers
- B. take the problem to the head of the organization
- C. take the problem to the person who gave him the assignment
- D. say nothing to anyone about his complaint

In answering this question, you should study each of the choices to find which is best. Consider choice "A" – Certainly an employee may discuss his complaint with fellow employees, but no change or improvement can result, and the complaint remains unresolved. Choice "B" is a poor choice since the head of the organization probably does not know what assignment you have been given, and taking your problem to him is known as "going over the head" of the supervisor. The supervisor, or person who made the assignment, is the person who can clarify it or correct any injustice. Choice "C" is, therefore, correct. To say nothing, as in choice "D," is unwise. Supervisors have and interest in knowing the problems employees are facing, and the employee is seeking a solution to his problem.

2. True/False

3. Matching Questions

Matching an answer from a column of choices within another column.

V. RECORDING YOUR ANSWERS

Computer terminals are used more and more today for many different kinds of exams.

For an examination with very few applicants, you may be told to record your answers in the test booklet itself. Separate answer sheets are much more common. If this separate answer sheet is to be scored by machine – and this is often the case – it is highly important that you mark your answers correctly in order to get credit.

VI. BEFORE THE TEST

YOUR PHYSICAL CONDITION IS IMPORTANT

If you are not well, you can't do your best work on tests. If you are half asleep, you can't do your best either. Here are some tips:

1) Get about the same amount of sleep you usually get. Don't stay up all night before the test, either partying or worrying—DON'T DO IT!
2) If you wear glasses, be sure to wear them when you go to take the test. This goes for hearing aids, too.
3) If you have any physical problems that may keep you from doing your best, be sure to tell the person giving the test. If you are sick or in poor health, you relay cannot do your best on any test. You can always come back and take the test some other time.

Common sense will help you find procedures to follow to get ready for an examination. Too many of us, however, overlook these sensible measures. Indeed, nervousness and fatigue have been found to be the most serious reasons why applicants fail to do their best on civil service tests. Here is a list of reminders:

- Begin your preparation early – Don't wait until the last minute to go scurrying around for books and materials or to find out what the position is all about.
- Prepare continuously – An hour a night for a week is better than an all-night cram session. This has been definitely established. What is more, a night a week for a month will return better dividends than crowding your study into a shorter period of time.
- Locate the place of the exam – You have been sent a notice telling you when and where to report for the examination. If the location is in a different town or otherwise unfamiliar to you, it would be well to inquire the best route and learn something about the building.
- Relax the night before the test – Allow your mind to rest. Do not study at all that night. Plan some mild recreation or diversion; then go to bed early and get a good night's sleep.
- Get up early enough to make a leisurely trip to the place for the test – This way unforeseen events, traffic snarls, unfamiliar buildings, etc. will not upset you.
- Dress comfortably – A written test is not a fashion show. You will be known by number and not by name, so wear something comfortable.
- Leave excess paraphernalia at home – Shopping bags and odd bundles will get in your way. You need bring only the items mentioned in the official notice you received; usually everything you need is provided. Do not bring reference books to the exam. They will only confuse those last minutes and be taken away from you when in the test room.

- Arrive somewhat ahead of time – If because of transportation schedules you must get there very early, bring a newspaper or magazine to take your mind off yourself while waiting.
- Locate the examination room – When you have found the proper room, you will be directed to the seat or part of the room where you will sit. Sometimes you are given a sheet of instructions to read while you are waiting. Do not fill out any forms until you are told to do so; just read them and be prepared.
- Relax and prepare to listen to the instructions
- If you have any physical problem that may keep you from doing your best, be sure to tell the test administrator. If you are sick or in poor health, you really cannot do your best on the exam. You can come back and take the test some other time.

VII. AT THE TEST

The day of the test is here and you have the test booklet in your hand. The temptation to get going is very strong. Caution! There is more to success than knowing the right answers. You must know how to identify your papers and understand variations in the type of short-answer question used in this particular examination. Follow these suggestions for maximum results from your efforts:

1) Cooperate with the monitor

The test administrator has a duty to create a situation in which you can be as much at ease as possible. He will give instructions, tell you when to begin, check to see that you are marking your answer sheet correctly, and so on. He is not there to guard you, although he will see that your competitors do not take unfair advantage. He wants to help you do your best.

2) Listen to all instructions

Don't jump the gun! Wait until you understand all directions. In most civil service tests you get more time than you need to answer the questions. So don't be in a hurry. Read each word of instructions until you clearly understand the meaning. Study the examples, listen to all announcements and follow directions. Ask questions if you do not understand what to do.

3) Identify your papers

Civil service exams are usually identified by number only. You will be assigned a number; you must not put your name on your test papers. Be sure to copy your number correctly. Since more than one exam may be given, copy your exact examination title.

4) Plan your time

Unless you are told that a test is a "speed" or "rate of work" test, speed itself is usually not important. Time enough to answer all the questions will be provided, but this does not mean that you have all day. An overall time limit has been set. Divide the total time (in minutes) by the number of questions to determine the approximate time you have for each question.

5) Do not linger over difficult questions

If you come across a difficult question, mark it with a paper clip (useful to have along) and come back to it when you have been through the booklet. One caution if you do this – be sure to skip a number on your answer sheet as well. Check often to be sure that you have not lost your place and that you are marking in the row numbered the same as the question you are answering.

6) Read the questions

Be sure you know what the question asks! Many capable people are unsuccessful because they failed to read the questions correctly.

7) Answer all questions

Unless you have been instructed that a penalty will be deducted for incorrect answers, it is better to guess than to omit a question.

8) Speed tests

It is often better NOT to guess on speed tests. It has been found that on timed tests people are tempted to spend the last few seconds before time is called in marking answers at random – without even reading them – in the hope of picking up a few extra points. To discourage this practice, the instructions may warn you that your score will be "corrected" for guessing. That is, a penalty will be applied. The incorrect answers will be deducted from the correct ones, or some other penalty formula will be used.

9) Review your answers

If you finish before time is called, go back to the questions you guessed or omitted to give them further thought. Review other answers if you have time.

10) Return your test materials

If you are ready to leave before others have finished or time is called, take ALL your materials to the monitor and leave quietly. Never take any test material with you. The monitor can discover whose papers are not complete, and taking a test booklet may be grounds for disqualification.

VIII. EXAMINATION TECHNIQUES

1) Read the general instructions carefully. These are usually printed on the first page of the exam booklet. As a rule, these instructions refer to the timing of the examination; the fact that you should not start work until the signal and must stop work at a signal, etc. If there are any special instructions, such as a choice of questions to be answered, make sure that you note this instruction carefully.

2) When you are ready to start work on the examination, that is as soon as the signal has been given, read the instructions to each question booklet, underline any key words or phrases, such as least, best, outline, describe and the like. In this way you will tend to answer as requested rather than discover on reviewing your paper that you listed without describing, that you selected the worst choice rather than the best choice, etc.

3) If the examination is of the objective or multiple-choice type – that is, each question will also give a series of possible answers: A, B, C or D, and you are called upon to select the best answer and write the letter next to that answer on your answer paper – it is advisable to start answering each question in turn. There may be anywhere from 50 to 100 such questions in the three or four hours allotted and you can see how much time would be taken if you read through all the questions before beginning to answer any. Furthermore, if you

come across a question or group of questions which you know would be difficult to answer, it would undoubtedly affect your handling of all the other questions.

4) If the examination is of the essay type and contains but a few questions, it is a moot point as to whether you should read all the questions before starting to answer any one. Of course, if you are given a choice – say five out of seven and the like – then it is essential to read all the questions so you can eliminate the two that are most difficult. If, however, you are asked to answer all the questions, there may be danger in trying to answer the easiest one first because you may find that you will spend too much time on it. The best technique is to answer the first question, then proceed to the second, etc.

5) Time your answers. Before the exam begins, write down the time it started, then add the time allowed for the examination and write down the time it must be completed, then divide the time available somewhat as follows:
   - If 3-1/2 hours are allowed, that would be 210 minutes. If you have 80 objective-type questions, that would be an average of 2-1/2 minutes per question. Allow yourself no more than 2 minutes per question, or a total of 160 minutes, which will permit about 50 minutes to review.
   - If for the time allotment of 210 minutes there are 7 essay questions to answer, that would average about 30 minutes a question. Give yourself only 25 minutes per question so that you have about 35 minutes to review.

6) The most important instruction is to read each question and make sure you know what is wanted. The second most important instruction is to time yourself properly so that you answer every question. The third most important instruction is to answer every question. Guess if you have to but include something for each question. Remember that you will receive no credit for a blank and will probably receive some credit if you write something in answer to an essay question. If you guess a letter – say "B" for a multiple-choice question – you may have guessed right. If you leave a blank as an answer to a multiple-choice question, the examiners may respect your feelings but it will not add a point to your score. Some exams may penalize you for wrong answers, so in such cases only, you may not want to guess unless you have some basis for your answer.

7) Suggestions
   a. Objective-type questions
      1. Examine the question booklet for proper sequence of pages and questions
      2. Read all instructions carefully
      3. Skip any question which seems too difficult; return to it after all other questions have been answered
      4. Apportion your time properly; do not spend too much time on any single question or group of questions
      5. Note and underline key words – all, most, fewest, least, best, worst, same, opposite, etc.
      6. Pay particular attention to negatives
      7. Note unusual option, e.g., unduly long, short, complex, different or similar in content to the body of the question
      8. Observe the use of "hedging" words – probably, may, most likely, etc.

9. Make sure that your answer is put next to the same number as the question
10. Do not second-guess unless you have good reason to believe the second answer is definitely more correct
11. Cross out original answer if you decide another answer is more accurate; do not erase until you are ready to hand your paper in
12. Answer all questions; guess unless instructed otherwise
13. Leave time for review

b. Essay questions
1. Read each question carefully
2. Determine exactly what is wanted. Underline key words or phrases.
3. Decide on outline or paragraph answer
4. Include many different points and elements unless asked to develop any one or two points or elements
5. Show impartiality by giving pros and cons unless directed to select one side only
6. Make and write down any assumptions you find necessary to answer the questions
7. Watch your English, grammar, punctuation and choice of words
8. Time your answers; don't crowd material

8) Answering the essay question

Most essay questions can be answered by framing the specific response around several key words or ideas. Here are a few such key words or ideas:

M's: manpower, materials, methods, money, management
P's: purpose, program, policy, plan, procedure, practice, problems, pitfalls, personnel, public relations

a. Six basic steps in handling problems:
1. Preliminary plan and background development
2. Collect information, data and facts
3. Analyze and interpret information, data and facts
4. Analyze and develop solutions as well as make recommendations
5. Prepare report and sell recommendations
6. Install recommendations and follow up effectiveness

b. Pitfalls to avoid
1. Taking things for granted – A statement of the situation does not necessarily imply that each of the elements is necessarily true; for example, a complaint may be invalid and biased so that all that can be taken for granted is that a complaint has been registered
2. Considering only one side of a situation – Wherever possible, indicate several alternatives and then point out the reasons you selected the best one
3. Failing to indicate follow up – Whenever your answer indicates action on your part, make certain that you will take proper follow-up action to see how successful your recommendations, procedures or actions turn out to be
4. Taking too long in answering any single question – Remember to time your answers properly

EXAMINATION SECTION

SPELLING

COMMENTARY

Spelling forms an integral part of tests of academic aptitude and achievement and of general and mental ability. Moreover, the spelling question is a staple of verbal and clerical tests in civil service entrance and promotional examinations.

Perhaps, the most rewarding way to learn to spell successfully is the direct, functional approach of learning to spell correctly, both orally and in writing, all words as they appear, both singly and in context.

In accordance with this positive method, the spelling question is presented here in "test" form, as it might appear on an actual examination.

The spelling question may appear on examinations in the following format:

> Four words are listed in each question. These are lettered A, B, C, and D. A fifth option, E, is also given, which always reads "none misspelled." The examinee is to select one of the five (lettered) choices: either A, B, C, or D if one of the words is misspelled, or item E, none misspelled, if all four words have been correctly spelled in the question.

SAMPLE QUESTIONS

The directions for this part are approximately as follows:

DIRECTIONS: Mark the space corresponding to the one MISSPELLED word in each of the following groups of words. If NO word is misspelled, mark the last space on the answer sheet.

SAMPLE O
- A. walk
- B. talk
- C. play
- D. dance
- E. *none misspelled*

Since none of the words is misspelled, E would be marked on the answer sheet.

SAMPLE OO
- A. seize
- B. yield
- C. define
- D. reccless
- E. *none misspelled*

Since "reccless" (correct spelling, reckless) has been misspelled, D would be marked on the answer. sheet

EXAMINATION SECTION
TEST 1

DIRECTIONS: In each of the following tests in this part, select the letter of the one MIS-SPELLED word in each of the following groups of words. If no word is misspelled, select the last item, letter E (none misspelled). *PRINT THE LETTER OF THE CORRECT ANSWER IN THE SPACE AT THE RIGHT.*

1. A. grateful   B. fundimental   C. census   1._____
   D. analysis   E. NONE MISSPELLED

2. A. installment   B. retrieve   C. concede   2._____
   D. dissapear   E. NONE MISSPELLED

3. A. accidentaly   B. dismissal   C. conscientious   3._____
   D. indelible   E. NONE MISSPELLED

4. A. perceive   B. carreer   C. anticipate   4._____
   D. acquire   E. NONE MISSPELLED

5. A. facility   B. reimburse   C. assortment   5._____
   D. guidance   E. NONE MISSPELLED

6. A. plentiful   B. across   C. advantagous   6._____
   D. similar   E. NONE MISSPELLED

7. A. omission   B. pamphlet   C. guarrantee   7._____
   D. repel   E. NONE MISSPELLED

8. A. maintenance   B. always   C. liable   8._____
   D. anouncement   E. NONE MISSPELLED

9. A. exaggerate   B. sieze   C. condemn   9._____
   D. commit   E. NONE MISSPELLED

10. A. pospone   B. altogether   C. grievance   10._____
    D. excessive   E. NONE MISSPELLED

11. A. arguing   B. correspondance   C. forfeit   11._____
    D. dissension   E. NONE MISSPELLED

12. A. occasion   B. description   C. prejudice   12._____
    D. elegible   E. NONE MISSPELLED

13. A. accomodate   B. initiative   C. changeable   13._____
    D. enroll   E. NONE MISSPELLED

14. A. temporary   B. insistent   C. benificial   14._____
    D. separate   E. NONE MISSPELLED

15. A. achieve   B. dissapoint   C. unanimous   15._____
    D. judgment   E. NONE MISSPELLED

16. A. proceed   B. publicly   C. sincerity   16._____
    D. successful   E. NONE MISSPELLED

17.	A. deceive D. repetitive	B. goverment E. *NONE MISSPELLED*	C. preferable		17.____
18.	A. emphasis D. optimistic	B. skillful E. *NONE MISSPELLED*	C. advisible		18.____
19.	A. tendency D. noticable	B. rescind E. *NONE MISSPELLED*	C. crucial		19.____
20.	A. privelege D. divisible	B. abbreviate E. *NONE MISSPELLED*	C. simplify		20.____

KEY (CORRECT ANSWERS)

1. B. fundamental
2. D. disappear
3. A. accidentally
4. B. career
5. E. None Misspelled
6. C. advantageous
7. C. guarantee
8. D. announcement
9. B. seize
10. A. postpone
11. B. correspondence
12. D. eligible
13. A. accommodate
14. C. beneficial
15. B. disappoint
16. E. None Misspelled
17. B. government
18. C. advisable
19. D. noticeable
20. A. privilege

TEST 2

DIRECTIONS: In each of the following tests in this part, select the letter of the one MIS-SPELLED word in each of the following groups of words. If no word is misspelled, select the last item, letter E (none misspelled). *PRINT THE LETTER OF THE CORRECT ANSWER IN THE SPACE AT THE RIGHT.*

1. A. typical B. descend C. summarize 1._____
   D. continuel E. *NONE MISSPELLED*

2. A. courageous B. recomend C. omission 2._____
   D. eliminate E. *NONE MISSPELLED*

3. A. compliment B. illuminate C. auxilary 3._____
   D. installation E. *NONE MISSPELLED*

4. A. preliminary B. aquainted C. syllable 4._____
   D. analysis E. *NONE MISSPELLED*

5. A. accustomed B. negligible C. interupted 5._____
   D. bulletin E. *NONE MISSPELLED*

6. A. summoned B. managment C. mechanism 6._____
   D. sequence E. *NONE MISSPELLED*

7. A. commitee B. surprise C. noticeable 7._____
   D. emphasize E. *NONE MISSPELLED*

8. A. occurrance B. likely C. accumulate 8._____
   D. grievance E. grievance

9. A. obstacle B. particuliar C. baggage 9._____
   D. fascinating E. *NONE MISSPELLED*

10. A. innumerable B. seize C. applicant 10._____
    D. dicionery E. *NONE MISSPELLED*

11. A. primary B. mechanic C. referred 11._____
    D. admissible E. *NONE MISSPELLED*

12. A. cessation B. beleif C. aggressive 12._____
    D. allowance E. *NONE MISSPELLED*

13. A. leisure B. authentic C. familiar 13._____
    D. contemptable E. *NONE MISSPELLED*

14. A. volume B. forty C. dilemma 14._____
    D. seldum E. *NONE MISSPELLED*

15. A. discrepancy B. aquisition C. exorbitant 15._____
    D. lenient E. *NONE MISSPELLED*

16. A. simultanous B. penetrate C. revision 16._____
    D. conspicuous E. *NONE MISSPELLED*

17. A. ilegible B. gracious C. profitable 17._____
    D. obedience E. *NONE MISSPELLED*

18. A. manufacturer   B. authorize   C. compelling   18.____
    D. pecular   E. *NONE MISSPELLED*

19. A. anxious   B. rehearsal   C. handicaped   19.____
    D. tendency   E. *NONE MISSPELLED*

20. A. meticulous   B. accompaning C. initiative 20.____
    D. shelves   E. *NONE MISSPELLED*

KEY (CORRECT ANSWERS)

1. D. continual
2. B. recommend
3. C. auxiliary
4. B. acquainted
5. C. interrupted
6. B. management
7. A. committee
8. A. occurrence
9. B. particular
10. D. dictionary
11. E. None Misspelled
12. B. belief
13. D. contemptible
14. D. seldom
15. B. acquisition
16. A. simultaneous
17. A. illegible
18. D. peculiar
19. C. handicapped
20. B. accompanying

TEST 3

DIRECTIONS: In each of the following tests in this part, select the letter of the one MIS-SPELLED word in each of the following groups of words. If no word is misspelled, select the last item, letter E (none misspelled). *PRINT THE LETTER OF THE CORRECT ANSWER IN THE SPACE AT THE RIGHT.*

1. A. grievous B. dilettante C. gibberish 1._____
   D. upbraid E. *NONE MISSPELLED*

2. A. embarrassing B. playright C. unmanageable 2._____
   D. symmetrical E. *NONE MISSPELLED*

3. A. sestet B. denouement C. liaison 3._____
   D. tattooing E. *NONE MISSPELLED*

4. A. prophesied B. soliliquy C. supersede 4._____
   D. hemorrhage E. *NONE MISSPELLED*

5. A. colossal B. renascent C. parallel 5._____
   D. omnivorous E. *NONE MISSPELLED*

6. A. passable B. dispensable C. deductable 6._____
   D. irreducible E. *NONE MISSPELLED*

7. A. guerrila B. carousal C. maneuver 7._____
   D. staid E. *NONE MISSPELLED*

8. A. maintenance B. mountainous C. sustenance 8._____
   D. gluttinous E. *NONE MISSPELLED*

9. A. holocaust B. irascible C. buccanneer 9._____
   D. mischievous E. *NONE MISSPELLED*

10. A. diphthong B. rhododendron C. inviegle 10._____
    D. shellacked E. *NONE MISSPELLED*

11. A. Phillipines B. currant C. dietitian 11._____
    D. coercion E. *NONE MISSPELLED*

12. A. courtesey B. buoyancy C. fiery 12._____
    D. shepherd E. *NONE MISSPELLED*

13. A. censor B. queue C. obbligato 13._____
    D. antartic E. *NONE MISSPELLED*

14. A. chrystal B. chrysanthemum C. chrysalis 14._____
    D. chrome E. *NONE MISSPELLED*

15. A. shreik B. siege C. sheik 15._____
    D. sieve E. *NONE MISSPELLED*

16. A. leisure B. gladioluses C. kindergarden 16._____
    D. tonnage E. *NONE MISSPELLED*

17. A. emminent B. imminent C. blatant 17._____
    D. privilege E. *NONE MISSPELLED*

18.	A. diphtheria D. sleight	B. collander E. *NONE MISSPELLED*	C. seize	18.___
19.	A. frolicking D. kohlrabi	B. caramel E. *NONE MISSPELLED*	C. germaine	19.___
20.	A. dispensable D. feasible	B. compatable E. *NONE MISSPELLED*	C. recommend	20.___

KEY (CORRECT ANSWERS)

1. E. None Misspelled
2. B. playwright
3. E. None Misspelled
4. B. soliloquy
5. E. None Misspelled
6. C. deductible
7. A. guerrilla
8. D. gluttonous
9. C. buccaneer
10. C. inveigle
11. A. Philippines
12. A. courtesy
13. D. antarctic
14. A. crystal
15. A. shriek
16. C. kindergarten
17. A. eminent
18. B. colander
19. C. germane
20. B. compatible

TEST 4

DIRECTIONS: In each of the following tests in this part, select the letter of the one MISSPELLED word in each of the following groups of words. If no word is misspelled, select the last item, letter E (none misspelled). *PRINT THE LETTER OF THE CORRECT ANSWER IN THE SPACE AT THE RIGHT.*

1. A. coercion B. rescission C. license 1.____
   D. prophecied E. *NONE MISSPELLED*

2. A. calcimine B. seive C. procedure 2.____
   D. poinsettia E. *NONE MISSPELLED*

3. A. entymology B. echoing C. subtly 3.____
   D. stupefy E. *NONE MISSPELLED*

4. A. mocassin B. assassin C. battalion 4.____
   D. despicable E. *NONE MISSPELLED*

5. A. moustache B. sovereignty C. drunkeness 5.____
   D. staccato E. *NONE MISSPELLED*

6. A. notoriety B. stereotype C. trellis 6.____
   D. Uraguay E. *NONE MISSPELLED*

7. A. hummock B. idiosyncrasy C. licentiate 7.____
   D. plagiarism E. *NONE MISSPELLED*

8. A. denim B. hyssop C. innoculate 8.____
   D. malevolent E. *NONE MISSPELLED*

9. A. boundaries B. corpulency C. gauge 9.____
   D. jingoes E. *NONE MISSPELLED*

10. A. assassin B. refulgeant C. sorghum 10.____
    D. suture E. *NONE MISSPELLED*

11. A. dormatory B. glimpse C. mediocre 11.____
    D. repetition E. *NONE MISSPELLED*

12. A. ambergris B. docility C. loquacious 12.____
    D. Pharoah E. *NONE MISSPELLED*

13. A. curriculum B. ninety-eighth C. occurrence 13.____
    D. repertoire E. *NONE MISSPELLED*

14. A. belladonna B. equable C. immersion 14.____
    D. naphtha E. *NONE MISSPELLED*

15. A. itinerary B. ptomaine C. similar 15.____
    D. solicetous E. *NONE MISSPELLED*

16. A. liquify B. mausoleum C. Philippines 16.____
    D. singeing E. *NONE MISSPELLED*

17. A. descendant B. harrassed C. implausible 17.____
    D. irreverence E. *NONE MISSPELLED*

9

2 (#4)

18. A. crystallize B. imperceptible C. isinglass 18.____
    D. precede E. *NONE MISSPELLED*

19. A. accommodate B. deferential C. gazeteer 19.____
    D. plenteous E. *NONE MISSPELLED*

20. A. aching B. buttress C. indigenous 20.____
    D. mischievous E. *NONE MISSPELLED*

KEY (CORRECT ANSWERS)

1. D. prophesied
2. B. sieve
3. A. entomology
4. A. moccasin
5. C. drunkenness
6. D. Uruguay
7. E. None Misspelled
8. C. inoculate
9. E. None Misspelled
10. B. refulgent
11. A. dormitory
12. D. Pharaoh
13. E. None Misspelled
14. E. None misspelled
15. D. solicitous
16. A. liquefy
17. B. harassed
18. E. None Misspelled
19. C. gazetteer
20. E. None Misspelled

TEST 5

DIRECTIONS: In each of the following tests in this part, select the letter of the one MISSPELLED word in each of the following groups of words. If no word is misspelled, select the last item, letter E (none misspelled). *PRINT THE LETTER OF THE CORRECT ANSWER IN THE SPACE AT THE RIGHT.*

1. A. comensurable   B. fracas   C. obeisance   1.____
   D. remittent   E. *NONE MISSPELLED*

2. A. defiance   B. delapidated   C. motley   2.____
   D. rueful   E. *NONE MISSPELLED*

3. A. demeanor   B. epoch   C. furtive   3.____
   D. parley   E. *NONE MISSPELLED*

4. A. disciples   B. influencial   C. nemesis   4.____
   D. poultry   E. *NONE MISSPELLED*

5. A. decision   B. encourage   C. incidental   5.____
   D. satyr   E. *NONE MISSPELLED*

6. A. collate   B. connivance   C. luxurient   6.____
   D. manageable   E. *NONE MISSPELLED*

7. A. constituencies   B. crocheted   C. foreclosure   7.____
   D. scintillating   E. *NONE MISSPELLED*

8. A. arraignment   B. assassination   C. carburator   8.____
   D. irrationally   E. *NONE MISSPELLED*

9. A. livelihood   B. noticeable   C. optomiatic   9.____
   D. psychology   E. *NONE MISSPELLED*

10. A. daub   B. massacre   C. repitition   10.____
    D. requiem   E. *NONE MISSPELLED*

11. A. adversary   B. beneficiary   C. cemetery   11.____
    D. desultory   E. *NONE MISSPELLED*

12. A. criterion   B. elicit   C. incredulity   12.____
    D. omnishient   E. *NONE MISSPELLED*

13. A. dining   B. fiery   C. incidentally   13.____
    D. rheumatism   E. *NONE MISSPELLED*

14. A. collaborator   B. gaudey   C. habilitation   14.____
    D. logician   E. *NONE MISSPELLED*

15. A. dirge   B. ogle   C. recumbent   15.____
    D. reminiscence   E. *NONE MISSPELLED*

16. A. conscientious   B. renunciation   C. inconvenient   16.____
    D. inoculate   E. *NONE MISSPELLED*

17. A. crystalline   B. scimitar   C. ecstacy   17.____
    D. vestigial   E. *NONE MISSPELLED*

2 (#5)

18. A. phlegmatic B. rhythm C. plebescite 18.____
    D. refectory E. *NONE MISSPELLED*

19. A. resilient B. resevoir C. recipient 19.____
    D. sobriety E. *NONE MISSPELLED*

20. A. privilege B. leige C. leisure 20.____
    D. basilisk E. *NONE MISSPELLED*

KEY (CORRECT ANSWERS)

1. A. commensurable
2. B. dilapidated
3. E. None Misspelled
4. B. influential
5. E. None Misspelled
6. C. luxuriant
7. E. None Misspelled
8. C. carburetor
9. C. optimistic
10. C. repetition
11. E. None Misspelled
12. D. omniscient
13. E. None Misspelled
14. B. gaudy
15. E. None Misspelled
16. E. None Misspelled
17. C. ecstasy
18. C. plebiscite
19. B. reservoir
20. B. liege

TEST 6

DIRECTIONS: In each of the following tests in this part, select the letter of the one MISSPELLED word in each of the following groups of words. If no word is misspelled, select the last item, letter E (none misspelled). *PRINT THE LETTER OF THE CORRECT ANSWER IN THE SPACE AT THE RIGHT.*

1. A. repellent   B. elliptical   C. paralelling   1._____
    D. colossal   E. *NONE MISSPELLED*

2. A. uproarious   B. grievous   C. armature   2._____
    D. tabular   E. *NONE MISSPELLED*

3. A. ammassed   B. embarrassed   C. promissory   3._____
    D. asymmetrical E. *NONE MISSPELLED*

4. A. maintenance B. correspondence C. benificence   4._____
    D. miasmic   E. *NONE MISSPELLED*

5. A. demurred   B. occurrence   C. temperament   5._____
    D. abhorrance   E. *NONE MISSPELLED*

6. A. proboscis   B. lucious   C. mischievous   6._____
    D. vilify   E. *NONE MISSPELLED*

7. A. feasable   B. divisible   C. permeable   7._____
    D. forcible   E. *NONE MISSPELLED*

8. A. courteous   B. venemous   C. heterogeneous   8._____
    D. lustrous   E. *NONE MISSPELLED*

9. A. millionaire B. mayonnaise   C. questionaire   9._____
    D. silhouette   E. *NONE MISSPELLED*

10. A. contemptible B. irreverent   C. illimitable   10._____
    D. inveigled   E. *NONE MISSPELLED*

11. A. prevalent   B. irrelavent   C. ecstasy   11._____
    D. auxiliary   E. *NONE MISSPELLED*

12. A. impeccable   B. raillery   C. precede   12._____
    D. occurrence   E. *NONE MISSPELLED*

13. A. patrolling   B. vignette   C. ninety   13._____
    D. surveilance E. *NONE MISSPELLED*

14. A. holocaust   B. incidently   C. weird   14._____
    D. canceled   E. *NONE MISSPELLED*

15. A. emmendation B. gratuitous   C. fissionable   15._____
    D. dilemma   E. *NONE MISSPELLED*

16. A. harass   B. innuendo   C. capilary   16._____
    D. pachyderm   E. *NONE MISSPELLED*

17. A. concomitant B. Lilliputian   C. sarcophagus   17._____
    D. melifluous   E. *NONE MISSPELLED*

18. A. interpolate B. disident C. venal 18.____
    D. inveigh E. *NONE MISSPELLED*

19. A. supercillious B. biennial C. gargantuan 19.____
    D. irresistible E. *NONE MISSPELLED*

20. A. conniving B. expedite C. inflammible 20.____
    D. incorruptible E. *NONE MISSPELLED*

KEY (CORRECT ANSWERS)

1. C. paralleling
2. E. None Misspelled
3. A. amassed
4. C. beneficence
5. D. abhorrence
6. B. luscious
7. A. feasible
8. B. venomous
9. C. questionnaire
10. E. None Misspelled
11. B. irrelevant
12. E. None Misspelled
13. D. surveillance
14. B. incidentally
15. A. emendation
16. C. capillary
17. D. mellifluous
18. B. dissident
19. A. supercilious
20. C. inflammable

TEST 7

DIRECTIONS: In each of the following tests in this part, select the letter of the one MISSPELLED word in each of the following groups of words. If no word is misspelled, select the last item, letter E (none misspelled). *PRINT THE LETTER OF THE CORRECT ANSWER IN THE SPACE AT THE RIGHT.*

1. A. torturous   B. omniscient   C. hymenial   1.____
    D. flaccid   E. *NONE MISSPELLED*

2. A. seige   B. seize   C. frieze   2.____
    D. grieve   E. *NONE MISSPELLED*

3. A. indispensible   B. euphony   C. victuals   3.____
    D. receptacle   E. *NONE MISSPELLED*

4. A. schism   B. fortissimo   C. innocuous 4.____
    D. epicurian   E. *NONE MISSPELLED*

5. A. sustenance B. vilefy   C. maintenance 5.____
    D. rarefy   E. *NONE MISSPELLED*

6. A. desiccated B. alleviate   C. beneficence 6.____
    D. preponderance   E. *NONE MISSPELLED*

7. A. battalion   B. incubus   C. sacrilegious 7.____
    D. innert   E. *NONE MISSPELLED*

8. A. shiboleth   B. connoisseur C. potpourri   8.____
    D. dichotomy   E. *NONE MISSPELLED*

9. A. pamphlet   B. similar   C. parlament   9.____
    D. benefited   E. *NONE MISSPELLED*

10. A. genealogy   B. tyrannical   C. diletante   10.____
    D. abhorrence E. *NONE MISSPELLED*

11. A. effeminate B. concensus   C. agglomeration 11.____
    D. fission   E. *NONE MISSPELLED*

12. A. narcissus   B. lyceum   C. odissey   12.____
    D. peccadillo E. *NONE MISSPELLED*

13. A. stupefied   B. psychiatry   C. onerous   13.____
    D. frieze   E. *NONE MISSPELLED*

14. A. intelligible   B. semaphore   C. pronounciation   14.____
    D. albumen   E. *NONE MISSPELLED*

15. A. annihilate B. tyrannical   C. occurence   15.____
    D. allergy   E. *NONE MISSPELLED*

16. A. gauging   B. probossis   C. specimen   16.____
    D. its   E. *NONE MISSPELLED*

17. A. diphthong   B. connoisseur C. iresistible 17.____
    D. dilemma   E. *NONE MISSPELLED*

18. A. affect B. baccillus C. beige 18.____
    D. seize E. *NONE MISSPELLED*

19. A. apostasy B. sustenance C. synonym 19.____
    D. epigrammatic E. *NONE MISSPELLED*

20. A. discernable B. consul C. efflorescence 20.____
    D. complement E. *NONE MISSPELLED*

KEY (CORRECT ANSWERS)

1. C. hymeneal
2. A. siege
3. A. indispensable
4. D. epicurean
5. B. vilify
6. E. None Misspelled
7. D. inert
8. A. shibboleth
9. C. parliament
10. C. dilettante
11. B. consensus
12. C. odyssey
13. E. None Misspelled
14. C. pronunciation
15. C. occurrence
16. B. proboscis
17. C. irresistible
18. B. bacillus
19. E. None Misspelled
20. A. discernible

TEST 8

DIRECTIONS: In each of the following tests in this part, select the letter of the one MISSPELLED word in each of the following groups of words. If no word is misspelled, select the last item, letter E (none misspelled). *PRINT THE LETTER OF THE CORRECT ANSWER IN THE SPACE AT THE RIGHT.*

1. A. righteous B. seafareing C. colloquial 1.____
   D. contumely E. *NONE MISSPELLED*

2. A. sanitarium B. vicissitude C. mischievious 2.____
   D. chlorophyll E. *NONE MISSPELLED*

3. A. captain B. theirs C. asceticism 3.____
   D. acquiesced E. *NONE MISSPELLED*

4. A. across B. her's C. democracy 4.____
   D. signature E. *NONE MISSPELLED*

5. A. villain B. vacillate C. imposter 5.____
   D. temperament E. *NONE MISSPELLED*

6. A. idyllic B. volitile C. obloquy 6.____
   D. emendation E. *NONE MISSPELLED*

7. A. heinous B. sattelite C. dissident 7.____
   D. ephemeral E. *NONE MISSPELLED*

8. A. ennoble B. shellacked C. vilify 8.____
   D. indissoluble E. *NONE MISSPELLED*

9. A. argueing B. intrepid C. papyrus 9.____
   D. foulard E. *NONE MISSPELLED*

10. A. guttural B. acknowleging C. isosceles 10.____
    D. assonance E. *NONE MISSPELLED*

11. A. shoeing B. exorcise C. development 11.____
    D. irreperable E. *NONE MISSPELLED*

12. A. counseling B. cancellation C. kidnapped 12.____
    D. repellant E. *NONE MISSPELLED*

13. A. disatisfy B. misstep C. usually 13.____
    D. gregarious E. *NONE MISSPELLED*

14. A. unparalleled B. beggar C. embarrass 14.____
    D. ecstacy E. *NONE MISSPELLED*

15. A. descendant B. poliomyelitis C. privilege 15.____
    D. tragedy E. *NONE MISSPELLED*

16. A. nullify B. siderial C. salability 16.____
    D. irrelevant E. *NONE MISSPELLED*

17. A. paraphenalia B. apothecaries C. occurrence 17.____
    D. plagiarize E. *NONE MISSPELLED*

17

18.	A. asinine D. indispensable	B. dissonent E. *NONE MISSPELLED*		C. opossum		18.____
19.	A. orifice D. accommodate	B. deferrment E. *NONE MISSPELLED*		C. harass		19.____
20.	A. changeable D. dissatisfy	B. therefor E. *NONE MISSPELLED*		C. incidently		20.____

KEY (CORRECT ANSWERS)

1. B. seafaring
2. C. mischievous
3. E. None Misspelled
4. B. hers
5. C. impostor
6. B. volatile
7. B. satellite
8. E. None Misspelled
9. A. arguing
10. B. acknowledging
11. D. irreparable
12. D. repellent
13. A. dissatisfy
14. D. ecstasy
15. E. None Misspelled
16. B. sidereal
17. A. paraphernalia
18. B. dissonant
19. B. deferment
20. C. incidentally

TEST 9

DIRECTIONS: In each of the following tests in this part, select the letter of the one MISSPELLED word in each of the following groups of words. If no word is misspelled, select the last item, letter E (none misspelled). *PRINT THE LETTER OF THE CORRECT ANSWER IN THE SPACE AT THE RIGHT.*

1. A. irreparably B. lovable C. comparitively 1.____
   D. audible E. *NONE MISSPELLED*

2. A. vilify B. efflorescence C. sarcophagus 2.____
   D. sacreligious E. *NONE MISSPELLED*

3. A. picnicking B. proceedure C. hypocrisy 3.____
   D. seize E. *NONE MISSPELLED*

4. A. discomfit B. sapient C. exascerbate 4.____
   D. sarsaparilla E. *NONE MISSPELLED*

5. A. valleys B. maintainance C. abridgment 5.____
   D. reticence E. *NONE MISSPELLED*

6. A. idylic B. beneficent C. singeing 6.____
   D. asterisk E. *NONE MISSPELLED*

7. A. appropos B. violoncello C. peony 7.____
   D. mucilage E. *NONE MISSPELLED*

8. A. caterpillar B. silhouette C. rhapsody 8.____
   D. frieze E. *NONE MISSPELLED*

9. A. appendicitis B. vestigeal C. colonnade 9.____
   D. tortuous E. *NONE MISSPELLED*

10. A. omlet B. diphtheria C. highfalutin 10.____
    D. miniature E. *NONE MISSPELLED*

11. A. diorama B. sustanance C. disastrous 11.____
    D. conscious E. *NONE MISSPELLED*

12. A. inelegible B. irreplaceable C. dissatisfied 12.____
    D. procedural E. *NONE MISSPELLED*

13. A. contemptible B. sacrilegious C. proffessor 13.____
    D. privilege E. *NONE MISSPELLED*

14. A. inoculate B. diptheria C. gladioli 14.____
    D. hypocrisy E. *NONE MISSPELLED*

15. A. pessimism B. ecstasy C. furlough 15.____
    D. vulnerible E. *NONE MISSPELLED*

16. A. supersede B. moccasin C. recondite 16.____
    D. rhythmical E. *NONE MISSPELLED*

17. A. Adirondack B. Phillipines C. Czechoslovakia 17.____
    D. Cincinnati E. *NONE MISSPELLED*

18. A. weird   B. impromptu   C. guerrila   18.____
    D. spontaneously   E. *NONE MISSPELLED*

19. A. newstand   B. accidentally   C. tangible   19.____
    D. reservoir   E. *NONE MISSPELLED*

20. A. macaroni   B. mackerel   C. ukulele   20.____
    D. giutar   E. *NONE MISSPELLED*

KEY (CORRECT ANSWERS)

1. C. comparatively
2. D. sacrilegious
3. B. procedure
4. C. exacerbate
5. B. maintenance
6. A. idyllic
7. A. apropos
8. E. None Misspelled
9. B. vestigial
10. A. omelet
11. B. sustenance
12. A. ineligible
13. C. professor
14. B. diphtheria
15. D. vulnerable
16. E. None Misspelled
17. B. Philippines
18. C. guerrilla
19. A. newsstand
20. D. guitar

TEST 10

DIRECTIONS: In each of the following tests in this part, select the letter of the one MIS-SPELLED word in each of the following groups of words. If no word is misspelled, select the last item, letter E (none misspelled). *PRINT THE LETTER OF THE CORRECT ANSWER IN THE SPACE AT THE RIGHT.*

1. A. rescission B. sacrament C. hypocricy 1.____
   D. salable E. *NONE MISSPELLED*

2. A. rhythm B. foreboding C. withal 2.____
   D. consciousness E. *NONE MISSPELLED*

3. A. noticeable B. drunkenness C. frolicked 3.____
   D. abcess E. *NONE MISSPELLED*

4. A. supersede B. canoeing C. exorbitant 4.____
   D. vigilance E. *NONE MISSPELLED*

5. A. idiosyncrasy B. pantomine C. isosceles 5.____
   D. wintry E. *NONE MISSPELLED*

6. A. numbskull B. indispensable C. fatiguing 6.____
   D. gluey E. *NONE MISSPELLED*

7. A. dryly B. egregious C. recommend 7.____
   D. irresistable' E. *NONE MISSPELLED*

8. A. unforgettable B. mackeral C. perseverance 8.____
   D. rococo E. *NONE MISSPELLED*

9. A. mischievous B. tyranical C. desiccate 9.____
   D. battalion E. *NONE MISSPELLED*

10. A. accede B. ninth C. abyssmal 10.____
    D. commonalty E. *NONE MISSPELLED*

11. A. resplendent B. colonnade C. harass 11.____
    D. mimicking E. *NONE MISSPELLED*

12. A. dilletante B. pusillanimous C. grievance 12.____
    D. cataclysm E. *NONE MISSPELLED*

13. A. anomaly B. connoisseur C. feasable 13.____
    D. stationery E. *NONE MISSPELLED*

14. A. ennervated B. rescission C. vacillate 14.____
    D. raucous E. *NONE MISSPELLED*

15. A. liquefy B. poniard C. truculent 15.____
    D. weird E. *NONE MISSPELLED*

16. A. existance B. lieutenant C. asinine 16.____
    D. parallelogram E. *NONE MISSPELLED*

17. A. protuberant B. nuisance C. instrumental 17.____
    D. resevoir E. *NONE MISSPELLED*

21

2 (#10)

18. A. sustenance B. pedigree C. supercillious 18.____
    D. clairvoyant E. *NONE MISSPELLED*

19. A. commingle B. bizarre C. gauge 19.____
    D. priviledge E. *NONE MISSPELLED*

20. A. analagous B. irresistible C. apparel 20.____
    D. hindrance E. *NONE MISSPELLED*

KEY (CORRECT ANSWERS)

1. C. hypocrisy
2. E. None Misspelled
3. D. abscess
4. E. None Misspelled
5. B. pantomime
6. A. numskull
7. D. irresistible
8. B. mackerel
9. B. tyrannical
10. C. abysmal
11. E. None Misspelled
12. A. dilettante
13. C. feasible
14. A. enervated
15. C. truculent
16. A. existence
17. D. reservoir
18. C. supercilious
19. D. privilege
20. A. analogous

TEST 11

DIRECTIONS: In each of the following tests in this part, select the letter of the one MIS-SPELLED word in each of the following groups of words. If no word is misspelled, select the last item, letter E (none misspelled). *PRINT THE LETTER OF THE CORRECT ANSWER IN THE SPACE AT THE RIGHT.*

1. A. impute   B. imparshal   C. immodest   1.____
   D. imminent   E. *NONE MISSPELLED*

2. A. cover   B. audit   C. adege   2.____
   D. adder   E. *NONE MISSPELLED*

3. A. promissory   B. maturity   C. severally   3.____
   D. accomodation   E. *NONE MISSPELLED*

4. A. superintendant   B. dependence   C. dependents   4.____
   D. entrance   E. *NONE MISSPELLED*

5. A. managable   B. navigable   C. passable   5.____
   D. laughable   E. *NONE MISSPELLED*

6. A. tolerance   B. circumference   C. insurance   6.____
   D. dominance   E. *NONE MISSPELLED*

7. A. diameter   B. tangent   C. paralell   7.____
   D. perimeter   E. *NONE MISSPELLED*

8. A. providential   B. personal   C. accidental   8.____
   D. diagonel   E. *NONE MISSPELLED*

9. A. ballast   B. ballustrade   C. allotment   9.____
   D. bourgeois   E. *NONE MISSPELLED*

10. A. diverse   B. pedantic   C. mishapen   10.____
    D. transient   E. *NONE MISSPELLED*

11. A. surgeon   B. sturgeon   C. luncheon   11.____
    D. stancheon   E. *NONE MISSPELLED*

12. A. pariah   B. estrang   C. conceive   12.____
    D. puncilious   E. *NONE MISSPELLED*

13. A. camouflage   B. serviceable   C. mischievious   13.____
    D. menace   E. *NONE MISSPELLED*

14. A. forefeit   B. halve   C. hundredth   14.____
    D. illusion   E. *NONE MISSPELLED*

15. A. filial   B. arras   C. pantomine   15.____
    D. filament   E. *NONE MISSPELLED*

16. A. llama   B. madrigal   C. martinet   16.____
    D. laxitive   E. *NONE MISSPELLED*

17. A. symtom   B. serum   C. antiseptic   17.____
    D. aromatic   E. *NONE MISSPELLED*

23

18. A. erasable B. irascible C. audable 18.____
    D. laudable E. *NONE MISSPELLED*

19. A. heroes B. folios C. sopranos 19.____
    D. cargos E. *NONE MISSPELLED*

20. A. latent B. goddess C. aisle 20.____
    D. whose E. *NONE MISSPELLED*

KEY (CORRECT ANSWERS)

1. B. impartial
2. C. adage
3. D. accommodation
4. A. superintendent
5. A. manageable
6. E. None Misspelled
7. C. parallel
8. D. diagonal
9. B. balustrade
10. C. misshapen
11. D. stanchion
12. B. estrange
13. C. mischievous
14. A. forfeit
15. C. pantomime
16. D. laxative
17. A. symptom
18. C. audible
19. D. cargoes
20. E. None Misspelled

TEST 12

DIRECTIONS: In each of the following tests in this part, select the letter of the one MISSPELLED word in each of the following groups of words. If no word is misspelled, select the last item, letter E (none misspelled). *PRINT THE LETTER OF THE CORRECT ANSWER IN THE SPACE AT THE RIGHT.*

1. A. coconut B. bustling C. abducter 1._____
   D. naphtha E. NONE MISSPELLED

2. A. seriatim B. quadruped C. diphthong 2._____
   D. concensus E. NONE MISSPELLED

3. A. sanction B. propencity C. parabola 3._____
   D. despotic E. NONE MISSPELLED

4. A. circumstantial B. imbroglio C. coalesce 4._____
   D. ductill E. NONE MISSPELLED

5. A. spontaneous B. superlitive C. telepathy 5._____
   D. thesis E. NONE MISSPELLED

6. A. adobe B. apellate C. billion 6._____
   D. chiropody E. NONE MISSPELLED

7. A. combatant B. helium C. esprit de corps 7._____
   D. debillity E. NONE MISSPELLED

8. A. iota B. gopher C. demoralize 8._____
   D. culvert E. NONE MISSPELLED

9. A. invideous B. gourmand C. embryo 9._____
   D. despicable E. NONE MISSPELLED

10. A. dispeptic B. dromedary C. dormant 10._____
    D. duress E. NONE MISSPELLED

11. A. spiggot B. suffrage C. technology 11._____
    D. thermostat E. NONE MISSPELLED

12. A. aberration B. antropology C. bayou 12._____
    D. cashew E. NONE MISSPELLED

13. A. ricochet B. poncho C. oposum 13._____
    D. melee E. NONE MISSPELLED

14. A. semester B. quadrent C. penchant 14._____
    D. mustang E. NONE MISSPELLED

15. A. rhetoric B. polygimy C. optimum 15._____
    D. mendicant E. NONE MISSPELLED

16. A. labyrint B. hegira C. ergot 16._____
    D. debenture E. NONE MISSPELLED

17. A. solvant B. radioactive C. photostat 17._____
    D. nominative E. NONE MISSPELLED

18. A. sporadic   B. excelsior   C. tenible   18.____
    D. thorax   E. NONE MISSPELLED

19. A. mischievous   B. bouillon   C. asinine   19.____
    D. alien   E. NONE MISSPELLED

20. A. sanguinery   B. prolix   C. harangue   20.____
    D. minutia   E. NONE MISSPELLED

KEY (CORRECT ANSWERS)

1. C. abductor
2. D. consensus
3. B. propensity
4. D. ductile
5. B. superlative
6. B. appellate
7. D. debility
8. E. None Misspelled
9. A. invidious
10. A. dyspeptic
11. A. spigot
12. B. anthropology
13. C. opossum
14. B. quadrant
15. B. polygamy
16. A. labyrinth
17. A. solvent
18. C. tenable
19. E. None Misspelled
20. A. sanguinary

TEST 13

DIRECTIONS: In each of the following tests in this part, select the letter of the one MISSPELLED word in each of the following groups of words. If no word is misspelled, select the last item, letter E (none misspelled). *PRINT THE LETTER OF THE CORRECT ANSWER IN THE SPACE AT THE RIGHT.*

1. A. controvert B. cache C. auricle 1.____
   D. impromptu E. *NONE MISSPELLED*

2. A. labial B. heffer C. intrigue 2.____
   D. decagon E. *NONE MISSPELLED*

3. A. statistics B. syllable C. tenon 3.____
   D. tituler E. *NONE MISSPELLED*

4. A. lenient B. migraine C. embarras 4.____
   D. nepotism E. *NONE MISSPELLED*

5. A. lichen B. horoscope C. orthadox 5.____
   D. pageant E. *NONE MISSPELLED*

6. A. libretto B. humis C. fallacy 6.____
   D. dextrose E. *NONE MISSPELLED*

7. A. clinical B. alimoney C. bourgeois 7.____
   D. proverbial E. *NONE MISSPELLED*

8. A. dictator B. clipper C. braggadoccio 8.____
   D. assuage E. *NONE MISSPELLED*

9. A. reverence B. hydraulic C. felon 9.____
   D. diaphram E. *NONE MISSPELLED*

10. A. retrobution B. polyp C. optician 10.____
    D. mentor E. *NONE MISSPELLED*

11. A. resonant B. helicopter C. rejoicing 11.____
    D. decisive E. *NONE MISSPELLED*

12. A. renigade B. restitution C. faculty 12.____
    D. devise E. *NONE MISSPELLED*

13. A. solicitors B. gratuitous C. spherical 13.____
    D. crusible E. *NONE MISSPELLED*

14. A. spongy B. ramify C. pica 14.____
    D. noxtious E. *NONE MISSPELLED*

15. A. automaton B. cadence C. consummate 15.____
    D. ancillery E. *NONE MISSPELLED*

16. A. magnanimous B. iminent C. tonsillitis 16.____
    D. dowager E. *NONE MISSPELLED*

17. A. aerial B. apprehend C. bilinear 17.____
    D. transum E. *NONE MISSPELLED*

18. A. vacuum B. idiom C. veriety 18.____
    D. warbler E. *NONE MISSPELLED*

19. A. zephyr B. rarify C. physiology 19.____
    D. nonpareil E. *NONE MISSPELLED*

20. A. risque B. posterity C. opus 20.____
    D. meridian E. *NONE MISSPELLED*

KEY (CORRECT ANSWERS)

1. E. None Misspelled
2. B. heifer
3. D. titular
4. C. embarrass
5. C. orthodox
6. B. humus
7. B. alimony
8. C. braggadocio
9. D. diaphragm
10. A. retribution
11. E. None Misspelled
12. A. renegade
13. D. crucible
14. D. noxious
15. D. ancillary
16. B. imminent
17. D. transom
18. C. variety
19. B. rarefy
20. D. meridian

TEST 14

DIRECTIONS: In each of the following tests in this part, select the letter of the one MIS-SPELLED word in each of the following groups of words. If no word is misspelled, select the last item, letter E (none misspelled). *PRINT THE LETTER OF THE CORRECT ANSWER IN THE SPACE AT THE RIGHT.*

1. A. pygmy B. seggregation C. clayey 1.____
   D. homogeneous E. *NONE MISSPELLED*

2. A. homeopathy B. predelection C. hindrance 2.____
   D. guillotine E. *NONE MISSPELLED*

3. A. cumulative B. dandelion C. incission 3.____
   D. malpractice E. *NONE MISSPELLED*

4. A. paradise B. allegiance C. frustrate 4.____
   D. impecunious E. *NONE MISSPELLED*

5. A. licquor B. mousse C. exclamatory 5.____
   D. disciple E. *NONE MISSPELLED*

6. A. lame B. winesome C. valvular 6.____
   D. unadvised E. *NONE MISSPELLED*

7. A. Terre Haute B. Cyrano de Bergerac C. Stamboul 7.____
   D. Roosvelt E. *NONE MISSPELLED*

8. A. perambulator B. ruminate C. litturgy 8.____
   D. staple E. *NONE MISSPELLED*

9. A. hectic B. inpregnate C. otter 9.____
   D. muscat E. *NONE MISSPELLED*

10. A. lighterage B. lumbar C. insurence 10.____
    D. monsoon E. *NONE MISSPELLED*

11. A. lethal B. iliterateness C. manifold 11.____
    D. minuet E. *NONE MISSPELLED*

12. A. forfeit B. halve C. hundredth 12.____
    D. illusion E. *NONE MISSPELLED*

13. A. dissolute B. conundrum C. fallacious 13.____
    D. descrimination E. *NONE MISSPELLED*

14. A. diva B. codicile C. expedient 14.____
    D. garrison E. *NONE MISSPELLED*

15. A. filial B. arras C. pantomine 15.____
    D. filament E. *NONE MISSPELLED*

16. A. inveigle B. paraphenalia C. archivist 16.____
    D. complexion E. *NONE MISSPELLED*

17. A. dessicate B. ambidextrous C. meritorious 17.____
    D. revocable E. *NONE MISSPELLED*

18.	A. queue D. binnocular		B. isthmus E. *NONE MISSPELLED*		C. committal	18.____
19.	A. changeable D. japanned		B. abbreviating E. *NONE MISSPELLED*		C. regretable	19.____
20.	A. Saskechewan D. Apennines		B. Bismarck E. *NONE MISSPELLED*		C. Albuquerque	20.____

KEY (CORRECT ANSWERS)

1. B. segregation
2. B. predilection
3. C. incision
4. E. None Misspelled
5. A. liquor
6. B. winsome
7. D. Roosevelt
8. C. liturgy
9. B. impregnate
10. C. insurance
11. B. illiterateness
12. E. None Misspelled
13. D. discrimination
14. B. codicil
15. C. pantomime
16. B. paraphernalia
17. A. desiccate
18. D. binocular
19. C. regrettable
20. A. Saskatchewan

TEST 15

DIRECTIONS: In each of the following tests in this part, select the letter of the one MISSPELLED word in each of the following groups of words. If no word is misspelled, select the last item, letter E (none misspelled). *PRINT THE LETTER OF THE CORRECT ANSWER IN THE SPACE AT THE RIGHT.*

1. A. culinery B. millinery C. humpbacked 1.____
   D. improvise E. *NONE MISSPELLED*

2. A. Brittany B. embarrassment C. coifure 2.____
   D. leveled E. *NONE MISSPELLED*

3. A. minnion B. aborgine C. antagonism 3.____
   D. arabesque E. *NONE MISSPELLED*

4. A. tractible B. camouflage C. permanent 4.____
   D. dextrous E. *NONE MISSPELLED*

5. A. inequitous B. kilowatt C. weasel 5.____
   D. lunging E. *NONE MISSPELLED*

6. A. palatable B. odious C. motif 6.____
   D. Maltese E. *NONE MISSPELLED*

7. A. Beau Brummel B. Febuary C. Bedouin 7.____
   D. Damascus E. *NONE MISSPELLED*

8. A. llama B. madrigal C. illitive 8.____
   D. marlin E. *NONE MISSPELLED*

9. A. babboon B. dossier C. esplanade 9.____
   D. frontispiece E. *NONE MISSPELLED*

10. A. thrashing B. threshing C. atavism 10.____
    D. artifect E. *NONE MISSPELLED*

11. A. ballast B. ballustrade C. allotment 11.____
    D. bourgeois E. *NONE MISSPELLED*

12. A. amenuensis B. saccharine C. hippopotamus 12.____
    D. rhinoceros E. *NONE MISSPELLED*

13. A. maintenance B. bullion C. khaki 13.____
    D. libarian E. *NONE MISSPELLED*

14. A. diverse B. pedantic C. mishapen 14.____
    D. transient E. *NONE MISSPELLED*

15. A. exhilirate B. avaunt C. avocado 15.____
    D. avocation E. *NONE MISSPELLED*

16. A. narcotic B. flippancy C. daffodil 16.____
    D. narcisus E. *NONE MISSPELLED*

17. A. inflamation B. disfranchisement C. surmise 17.____
    D. adviser E. *NONE MISSPELLED*

2 (#15)

18. A. syphon B. inquiry C. shanghaied 18.____
    D. collapsible E. *NONE MISSPELLED*

19. A. occassionally B. antecedence C. reprehensible 19.____
    D. inveigh E. *NONE MISSPELLED*

20. A. crescendos B. indispensible C. mosquitoes 20.____
    D. impeccable E. *NONE MISSPELLED*

KEY (CORRECT ANSWERS)

1. A. culinary
2. C. coiffure
3. A. minion
4. A. tractable
5. A. iniquitous
6. E. None Misspelled
7. B. February
8. D. illative
9. A. baboon
10. D. artifact
11. B. balustrade
12. A. amanuensis
13. D. librarian
14. C. misshapen
15. A. exhilarate
16. D. narcissus
17. A. inflammation
18. E. None Misspelled
19. A. occasionally
20. B. indispensable

TESTS IN SPELLING

EXAMINATION SECTION
TEST 1

DIRECTIONS: In each question of the following tests, select the letter of the one MIS-SPELLED word in each of the listed groups of five (5) words. *PRINT THE LETTER OF THE CORRECT ANSWER IN THE SPACE AT THE RIGHT.*

1.	A.	break	B.	scenary	C.	business	D.	arouse	E.	religious	1.____
2.	A.	rinsed	B.	height	C.	jewel	D.	furtile	E.	doesn't	2.____
3.	A.	perform	B.	divide	C.	apologize	D.	occasion	E.	acheive	3.____
4.	A.	asending	B.	benefit	C.	disappear	D.	operate	E.	grammar	4.____
5.	A.	forty	B.	precede	C.	annuel	D.	parable	E.	curiosity	5.____
6.	A.	irritable	B.	stupefy	C.	gaseous	D.	millionair	E.	luscious	6.____
7.	A.	invincible	B.	Slav	C.	supersede	D.	haddock	E.	fatigueing	7.____
8.	A.	scissors	B.	explanatory	C.	bituminus	D.	heifer	E.	cessation	8.____
9.	A.	caramel	B.	Wisconsin	C.	acquarium	D.	sterilize	E.	pseudonym	9.____
10.	A.	precipise	B.	knapsack	C.	brilliance	D.	challenge	E.	decrepit	10.____
11.	A.	certificate	B.	ajourn	C.	apparel	D.	aggression	E.	symphony	11.____
12.	A.	Norwegian	B.	constent	C.	interruption	D.	wouldn't	E.	article	12.____
13.	A.	heros	B.	logical	C.	guarantee	D.	imprison	E.	legitimate	13.____
14.	A.	happiness	B.	weird	C.	miscellaneous	D.	village	E.	arguement	14.____
15.	A.	wretched	B.	tendency	C.	controversiel	D.	arbitrary	E.	denial	15.____
16.	A.	lonliness	B.	safeguard	C.	pilot	D.	chiefs	E.	obstacle	16.____
17.	A.	shining	B.	professional	C.	scheme	D.	excitment	E.	expectancy	17.____
18.	A.	negative	B.	editorial	C.	clothe	D.	economize	E.	suprising	18.____
19.	A.	illegal	B.	opinion	C.	discription	D.	rationalize	E.	picnicking	19.____
20.	A.	circuit	B.	sponser	C.	exasperate	D.	volume	E.	valuable	20.____

KEY (CORRECT ANSWERS)

1. B. scenery
2. D. fertile
3. E. achieve
4. A. ascending
5. C. annual
6. D. millionaire
7. E. fatiguing
8. C. bituminous
9. C. aquarium
10. A. precipice
11. B. adjourn
12. B. constant
13. A. heroes
14. E. argument
15. C. controversial
16. A. loneliness
17. D. excitement
18. E. surprising
19. C. description
20. B. sponsor

TEST 2

DIRECTIONS: In each question of the following tests, select the letter of the one MIS-SPELLED word in each of the listed groups of five (5) words. *PRINT THE LETTER OF THE CORRECT ANSWER IN THE SPACE AT THE RIGHT*

1. A. procession   B. performance   C. poize   D. allied   E. discipline   1.____
2. A. advocate   B. saleries   C. commercial   D. expense   E. forcibly   2.____
3. A. enormous   B. enterprise   C. florist   D. humilliate   E. careful   3.____
4. A. treachery   B. bolstor   C. simplify   D. revelation   E. reciprocal   4.____
5. A. witness   B. derisive   C. typewriter   D. relative   E. medecine   5.____
6. A. betrayel   B. forsaken   C. impetuous   D. finesse   E. recognize   6.____
7. A. forcast   B. pastime   C. several   D. ridiculous   E. cleanliness   7.____
8. A. correspond   B. conceited   C. implies   D. receptacle   E. amatuer   8.____
9. A. captain   B. definitely   C. credited   D. cordially   E. couragous   9.____
10. A. parallel   B. various   C. obnoxious   D. assurence   E. grateful   10.____
11. A. feirce   B. ascent   C. allies   D. doctor   E. coming   11.____
12. A. hopeless   B. absense   C. foretell   D. certain   E. similar   12.____
13. A. advise   B. muscle   C. manual   D. provocation E. copywright   13.____
14. A. behooves   B. reservoir   C. frostbiten   D. squalor   E. ambuscade   14.____
15. A. systematic B. precious   C. tremenduous D. insulation   E. brilliant   15.____
16. A. significant B. jurisdiction C. libel   D. monkies   E. legacy   16.____
17. A. delicatessen B. occupansy   C. gorgeous   D. consolation E. anxiety   17.____
18. A. tyranny   B. perennial   C. catagory   D. inspector   E. confidential   18.____
19. A. symbol   B. formerly   C. warring   D. caution   E. bankrupcy   19.____
20. A. aperture   B. cellaphane   C. diagnosis   D. intestinal   E. mahogany   20.____

KEY (CORRECT ANSWERS)

1. C. poise
2. B. salaries
3. D. humiliate
4. B. bolster
5. E. medicine
6. A. betrayal
7. A. forecast
8. E. amateur
9. E. courageous
10. D. assurance
11. A. fierce
12. B. abscence
13. E. copyright
14. C. frostbitten
15. C. tremendous
16. D. monkeys
17. B. occupancy
18. C. category
19. E. bankruptcy
20. B. cellophane

TEST 3

DIRECTIONS: In each question of the following tests, select the letter of the one MISSPELLED word in each of the listed groups of five (5) words. *PRINT THE LETTER OF THE CORRECT ANSWER IN THE SPACE AT THE RIGHT.*

1. A. pitiful B. latter C. ommitted D. agreement E. reconcile 1.____
2. A. banaana B. routine C. likewise D. indecent E. habitually 2.____
3. A. relieve B. copys C. ninety D. crowded E. electoral 3.____
4. A. adviseable B. illustrative C. financial D. nevertheless E. chimneys 4.____
5. A. prisioner B. immediate C. statistics D. surgeon E. treachery 5.____
6. A. option B. extradite C. comparitive D. jealousy E. illusion 6.____
7. A. handicaped B. assurance C. sympathy D. speech E. dining 7.____
8. A. recommend B. carraige C. disapprove D. independent E. mortgage 8.____
9. A. systematic B. ingenuity C. tenet D. uncanny E. intrigueing 9.____
10. A. arduous B. hideous C. fervant D. companies E. breach 10.____
11. A. together B. attempt C. loyality D. innocent E. rinse 11.____
12. A. argueing B. emergency C. kindergarten D. religious E. schedule 12.____
13. A. society B. anticipate C. dissatisfy D. responsable E. temporary 13.____
14. A. chaufeur B. grammar C. planned D. dining room E. accurate 14.____
15. A. confidence B. maturity C. aspiration D. evasion E. insurance 15.____
16. A. unnecessary B. dirigible C. transparant D. similar E. appetite 16.____
17. A. regional B. slimy C. tumbler D. educator E. femenine 17.____
18. A. orchestration B. proclamation C. pretext D. rearmement E. invoice 18.____
19. A. fragrant B. independent C. halves D. parallel E. advantagous 19.____
20. A. championing B. conversion C. predominent D. puppet E. anarchist 20.____

KEY (CORRECT ANSWERS)

1. C. omitted
2. A. banana
3. B. copies
4. A. advisable
5. A. prisoner
6. C. comparative
7. A. handicapped
8. B. carriage
9. E. intriguing
10. C. fervent
11. C. loyalty
12. A. arguing
13. D. responsible
14. A. chauffeur
15. E. insurance
16. C. transparent
17. E. feminine
18. D. rearmament
19. E. advantageous
20. C. predominant

TEST 4

DIRECTIONS: In each question of the following tests, select the letter of the one MISSPELLED word in each of the listed groups of five (5) words. *PRINT THE LETTER OF THE CORRECT ANSWER IN THE SPACE AT THE RIGHT.*

1. A. wrist B. welfare C. necessity D. scenery E. tendancy 1.____
2. A. commiting B. accusation C. endurance D. agreeable E. excitable 2.____
3. A. despair B. surgury C. privilege D. appreciation E. journeying 3.____
4. A. cameos B. propaganda C. delicious D. heathen E. interupt 4.____
5. A. relieve B. disappear C. development D. matress E. ninety-nine 5.____
6. A. finally B. bulitin C. doctor D. desirable E. sincerely 6.____
7. A. wrest B. array C. auspices D. sacrafice E. generations 7.____
8. A. liquid B. vegetable C. silence D. familiar E. fasinate 8.____
9. A. tomato B. suspence C. leisure D. license E. permanent 9.____
10. A. characteristic B. soliciting C. repititious D. immediately E. extravagant 10.____
11. A. travel B. conductor C. equiping D. proposal E. twofold 11.____
12. A. philosopher B. minority C. managment D. emergency E. bibliography 12.____
13. A. constructive B. employee C. stalwart D. masterpeice E. theoretical 13.____
14. A. dissappoint B. volcanic C. illiterate D. myth E. superficial 14.____
15. A. totally B. penninsula C. sandwich D. ripening E. salvation 15.____
16. A. pastel B. aisle C. primarly D. journalistic E. diminished 16.____
17. A. warrier B. unification C. enamel D. defendant E. sustained 17.____
18. A. incidental B. lubricent C. conversion D. jurisdiction E. interpretation 18.____
19. A. auxilary B. boundaries C. session D. fabric E. ceiling 19.____
20. A. imperious B. depreciate C. rebutal D. wharf E. giddy 20.____

KEY (CORRECT ANSWERS)

1. E. tendency
2. A. committing
3. B. surgery
4. E. interrupt
5. D. mattress
6. B. bulletin
7. D. sacrifice
8. E. fascinate
9. B. suspense
10. C. repetitious
11. C. equipping
12. C. management
13. D. masterpiece
14. A. disappoint
15. B. peninsula
16. C. primarily
17. A. warrior
18. B. lubricant
19. A. auxiliary
20. C. rebuttal

TEST 5

DIRECTIONS: In each question of the following tests, select the letter of the one MIS-SPELLED word in each of the listed groups of five (5) words. *PRINT THE LETTER OF THE CORRECT ANSWER IN THE SPACE AT THE RIGHT.*

1. A. renewel B. charitable C. abrupt D. humankind E. strengthen 1.____
2. A. khaki B. survival C. laboratory D. intensefied E. stature 2.____
3. A. diesel B. cocoa C. alphabetti-cal D. visible E. overlaid 3.____
4. A. neutral B. ballot C. parallysis D. enterprise E. abnormal 4.____
5. A. ironical B. mountainous C. permissible D. carburetor E. blizard 5.____
6. A. penalty B. affidavit C. document D. notery E. valid 6.____
7. A. provocative B. apparition C. forfiet D. procedure E. requisite 7.____
8. A. terrifying B. museum C. minimum D. competitors E. efficiensy 8.____
9. A. hangar B. spokesman C. mustache D. cathederal E. pumpkin 9.____
10. A. guidance B. until C. usage D. loyalist E. prarie 10.____
11. A. obnoxious B. balancing C. squadron D. illicit E. clearence 11.____
12. A. timetable B. gymnasium C. humid D. disolve E. gracious 12.____
13. A. spiciness B. bibliography C. injunction D. mediator E. discriminate 13.____
14. A. endearing B. mannerism C. predecesser D. gardener E. instantaneous 14.____
15. A. shrewdness B. purified C. acceptable D. uniqueness E. corugated 15.____
16. A. baptize B. diversity C. parochial D. abandonning E. hypnosis 16.____
17. A. deteryorate B. priority C. cuddle D. shrivel E. narcotic 17.____
18. A. neutrality B. horseradish C. contemporaries D. inducement E. prelimnery 18.____
19. A. eventually B. disilusioned C. divine D. inimitable E. fraudulent 19.____
20. A. verticle B. musician C. tomatoes D. athletic E. decision 20.____

41

KEY (CORRECT ANSWERS)

1. A. renewal
2. D. intensified
3. C. alphabetical
4. C. paralysis
5. E. blizzard
6. D. notary
7. C. forfeit
8. E. efficiency
9. D. cathedral
10. E. prairie
11. E. clearance
12. D. dissolve
13. B. bibliography
14. C. predecessor
15. E. corrugated
16. D. abandoning
17. A. deteriorate
18. E. preliminary
19. B. disillusioned
20. A. vertical

TEST 6

DIRECTIONS: In each question of the following tests, select the letter of the one MISSPELLED word in each of the listed groups of five (5) words. *PRINT THE LETTER OF THE CORRECT ANSWER IN THE SPACE AT THE RIGHT.*

1. A. advising   B. recognize   C. seize   D. supply   E. tradegy   1.____
2. A. intensive   B. stationary   C. benifit   D. equipped   E. preferring   2.____
3. A. predjudice B. pervade   C. excel   D. capitol   E. chimneys   3.____
4. A. all right   B. ninty   C. cronies   D. nervous   E. separate   4.____
5. A. atheletic   B. queue   C. furl   D. schedule   E. abusing   5.____
6. A. skein   B. wholesome   C. witches   D. coherent   E. defenite   6.____
7. A. aggravate   B. counsel   C. deplorable   D. proficency   E. catarrh   7.____
8. A. suppressed B. lugubrious   C. pecuniary   D. boulevard   E. fourty-fourth   8.____
9. A. militarism B. pilot   C. crimnal   D. monotonous   E. tendency   9.____
10. A. prevalent B. berth   C. auxiliary   D. priveleges   E. women's   10.____
11. A. incurred   B. cieling   C. strengthen   D. carnage   E. typical   11.____
12. A. twins   B. year's   C. acutely   D. changible   E. facility   12.____
13. A. deliscious B. enormous   C. likeness   D. witnesses   E. commodity   13.____
14. A. scenes   B. enlargement C. discretion   D. acknowledging E. sesion   14.____
15. A. annum   B. strenuous   C. tretchery   D. infamy   E. opportune   15.____
16. A. marmelade B. loot   C. kinsman   D. crochet   E. hawser   16.____
17. A. fireman   B. glossary   C. tuition   D. dissapoint   E. refrigerator   17.____
18. A. inadequate B. municpal   C. bored   D. masonic   E. utilize   18.____
19. A. partisan   B. temporary   C. cawleflower   D. obstinacy   E. hyperbole   19.____
20. A. people's   B. spherical   C. foliage   D. everlasting   E. feesable   20.____

KEY (CORRECT ANSWERS)

1. E. tragedy
2. C. benefit
3. A. prejudice
4. B. ninety
5. A. athletic
6. E. definite
7. D. proficiency
8. E. forty-fourth
9. C. criminal
10. D. privileges
11. B. ceiling
12. D. changeable
13. A. delicious
14. E. session
15. C. treachery
16. A. marmalade
17. D. disappoint
18. B. municipal
19. C. cauliflower
20. E. feasible

TEST 7

DIRECTIONS: In each question of the following tests, select the letter of the one MISSPELLED word in each of the listed groups of five (5) words. *PRINT THE LETTER OF THE CORRECT ANSWER IN THE SPACE AT THE RIGHT.*

1. A. inferred B. whisle C. jovial D. conscript E. gracious 1.____
2. A. tantalizing B. ominous C. conductor D. duchess E. telegram 2.____
3. A. reconcile B. primitive C. sausy D. quinine E. cede 3.____
4. A. immagine B. viaduct C. chisel D. Saturn E. currant 4.____
5. A. amplify B. greace C. cholera D. perilous E. theology 5.____
6. A. pursevere B. deodorize C. ligament D. illuminate E. dropsy 6.____
7. A. legible B. frivolously C. precious D. rezemblence E. congeal 7.____
8. A. intramural B. epidemic C. germicide D. anonymous E. acurracy 8.____
9. A. affable B. hazard C. combustable D. lacquer E. stationary 9.____
10. A. sagacious B. interpreter C. poultise D. dinosaur E. dismal 10.____
11. A. acknowledging B. deligate C. foliage D. staid E. loot 11.____
12. A. gardian B. losing C. notwithstanding D. worlds E. typhoid 12.____
13. A. medal B. utilize C. efficiency D. apricot E. soliceting 13.____
14. A. museum B. Christian C. possesion D. occasional E. bored 14.____
15. A. capitol B. sieze C. premises D. fragrance E. tonnage 15.____
16. A. requisition B. faculties C. canon D. chaufur E. stomach 16.____
17. A. solemn B. ascertain C. I'll D. chef E. delinquant 17.____
18. A. parliments B. distributor C. voluntary D. lovable E. counsel 18.____
19. A. morale B. democrat C. rhumatism D. dormitory E. leased 19.____
20. A. screech B. missapropriating C. courtesies D. wretched E. furlough 20.____

KEY (CORRECT ANSWERS)

1. B. whistle
2. E. telegram
3. C. saucy
4. A. imagine
5. B. grease
6. A. persevere
7. D. resemblance
8. E. accuracy
9. C. combustible
10. C. poultice
11. B. delegate
12. A. guardian
13. E. soliciting
14. C. possession
15. B. seize
16. D. chauffeur
17. E. delinquent
18. A. parliaments
19. C. rheumatism
20. B. misappropriating

TEST 8

DIRECTIONS: In each question of the following tests, select the letter of the one MISSPELLED word in each of the listed groups of five (5) words. *PRINT THE LETTER OF THE CORRECT ANSWER IN THE SPACE AT THE RIGHT.*

1.	A.	typhoid	B.	tarriff	C.	visible	D.	accent	E.	countries	1._____
2.	A.	dizzy	B.	leggings	C.	steak	D.	compaine	E.	interior	2._____
3.	A.	profit	B.	tiranny	C.	shocked	D.	response	E.	innocent	3._____
4.	A.	freshman	B.	vague	C.	larsiny	D.	ignorant	E.	worrying	4._____
5.	A.	disatesfied	B.	jealous	C.	unfortunately	D.	economical	E.	lettuce	5._____
6.	A.	based	B.	primarily	C.	condemned	D.	accompanied	E.	dupped	6._____
7.	A.	superntendant	B.	veil	C.	congenial	D.	quantities	E.	ere	7._____
8.	A.	unanimous	B.	dessert	C.	undoubtedly	D.	kolera	E.	nuisance	8._____
9.	A.	woman's	B.	bulletin	C.	'tis	D.	Pullman	E.	envellop	9._____
10.	A.	initiate	B.	guardian	C.	pagent	D.	wretched	E.	adieu	10._____
11.	A.	continually	B.	guild	C.	vegtable	D.	vague	E.	patience	11._____
12.	A.	desease	B.	parole	C.	gallery	D.	awkward	E.	you'd	12._____
13.	A.	border	B.	warrant	C.	operated	D.	economics	E.	ilegal	13._____
14.	A.	fatal	B.	agatation	C.	obliged	D.	studying	E.	resignation	14._____
15.	A.	ammendment	B.	promptness	C.	glimpse	D.	canon	E.	tract	15._____
16.	A.	wholly	B.	apricot	C.	destruction	D.	pappal	E.	leisure	16._____
17.	A.	issuing	B.	rabbid	C.	unauthorized	D.	parasite	E.	khaki	17._____
18.	A.	nowadays	B.	courtesies	C.	negotiate	D.	gaurdian	E.	derrick	18._____
19.	A.	partisan	B.	seanse	C.	vacancy	D.	fragrance	E.	corps	19._____
20.	A.	equipped	B.	nuisance	C.	phrenoligist	D.	foreign	E.	insignia	20._____

KEY (CORRECT ANSWERS)

1. B. tariff
2. D. company
3. B. tyranny
4. C. larceny
5. A. dissatisfied
6. E. duped
7. A. superintendent
8. D. cholera
9. E. envelope
10. C. pageant
11. C. vegetable
12. A. disease
13. E. illegal
14. B. agitation
15. A. amendment
16. D. papal
17. B. rabid
18. D. guardian
19. B. seance
20. C. phrenologist

TEST 9

DIRECTIONS: In each question of the following tests, select the letter of the one MISSPELLED word in each of the listed groups of five (5) words. *PRINT THE LETTER OF THE CORRECT ANSWER IN THE SPACE AT THE RIGHT.*

1. A. frightfully B. mantain C. post office D. specific E. bachelor 1.____
2. A. cease B. turkeys C. woman's D. hustling E. weild 2.____
3. A. expedition B. valuoble C. typhoid D. grapevines E. advice 3.____
4. A. echoes B. absoluty C. foggy D. wretched E. Sabbath 4.____
5. A. screech B. motorist C. congresionel D. utilize E. eligible 5.____
6. A. quizzes B. coarse C. aquaintence D. exhibition E. totally 6.____
7. A. principle B. transferring C. statutes D. here's E. sergeon 7.____
8. A. porcilane B. primeval C. suite D. unauthorized E. declension 8.____
9. A. commodity B. mischevious C. galvanized D. ordinance E. tuition 9.____
10. A. Christian B. fraternity C. accompanying D. disernable E. inadequate 10.____
11. A. subsidy B. inference C. chronicle D. purchace E. adroit 11.____
12. A. resources B. cargoes C. oponent D. disbelief E. treasurer 12.____
13. A. origional B. provincial C. knuckle D. ridiculous E. ecstasy 13.____
14. A. attitude B. soloes C. occurred D. policies E. technique 14.____
15. A. opinionated B. quantity C. systematic D. drought E. confidencial 15.____
16. A. interim B. idleness C. accesion D. elite E. fungi 16.____
17. A. inarticulate B. servitude C. ejaculate D. herewith E. preceedence 17.____
18. A. experimental B. minority C. cultural D. expedient E. penant 18.____
19. A. apparently B. criticism C. justification D. physican E. simultaneous 19.____
20. A. accidentally B. overule C. unintentional D. talented E. maturation 20.____

KEY (CORRECT ANSWERS)

1. B. maintain
2. E. wield
3. B. valuable
4. B. absolutely
5. C. congressional
6. C. acquaintance
7. E. surgeon
8. A. porcelain
9. B. mischievous
10. D. discernible
11. D. purchase
12. C. opponent
13. A. original
14. B. solos
15. E. confidential
16. C. accession
17. E. precedence
18. E. pennant
19. D. physician
20. B. overrule

TEST 10

DIRECTIONS: In each question of the following tests, select the letter of the one MIS-SPELLED word in each of the listed groups of five (5) words. *PRINT THE LETTER OF THE CORRECT ANSWER IN THE SPACE AT THE RIGHT.*

1. A. liabillity B. capacity C. guidance D. illegible E. expedient 1.____
2. A. debris B. apetite C. mosquitoes D. vessal E. yacht 2.____
3. A. tireless B. feindish C. recruit D. swarthy E. sandal 3.____
4. A. redouble B. wizard C. murdurer D. hindrance E. syncope 4.____
5. A. equalize B. turbulent C. repetitive D. corronation E. statistical 5.____
6. A. remittance B. sensitivity C. fatality D. soprano E. inconveniance 6.____
7. A. fraternity B. plebeian C. inteligible D. trickster E. expeditionary 7.____
8. A. gasous B. consistency C. brooches D. magistrate E. translucent 8.____
9. A. lightning B. persistent C. cynical D. musician E. recipricate 9.____
10. A. commodity B. fictitous C. rabid D. gaiety E. couldn't 10.____
11. A. visible B. creditor C. paradice D. infinite E. questionnaire 11.____
12. A. existence B. disarming C. endorsement D. commercal E. trigger 12.____
13. A. aluminum B. stuning C. allowance D. irate E. pleasantry 13.____
14. A. cipher B. colloquial C. envoy D. pursued E. writting 14.____
15. A. insurable B. benign C. influentual D. sophomore E. casualty 15.____
16. A. presentiment B. theological C. anatamy D. eccentricity E. amphibious 16.____
17. A. embargo B. vocalize C. recommend D. confering E. remunerate 17.____
18. A. tangent B. fickel C. circuit D. mathematics E. vegetarian 18.____
19. A. unscheduled B. declension C. secretariat D. forsight E. enamel 19.____
20. A. hygienic B. arrogant C. disbanded D. census E. memorandem 20.____

KEY (CORRECT ANSWERS)

1. A. liability
2. B. appetite
3. B. fiendish
4. C. murderer
5. D. coronation
6. E. inconvenience
7. C. intelligible
8. A. gaseous
9. E. reciprocate
10. B. fictitious
11. C. paradise
12. D. commercial
13. B. stunning
14. E. writing
15. C. influential
16. C. anatomy
17. D. conferring
18. B. fickle
19. D. foresight
20. E. memorandum

TESTS IN SPELLING

EXAMINATION SECTION
TEST 1

DIRECTIONS: In each question of the following tests, select the letter of the one MIS-SPELLED word in each of the listed groups of five (5) words. *PRINT THE LETTER OF THE CORRECT ANSWER IN THE SPACE AT THE RIGHT.*

1. A. barely B. assigned C. mechanical D. concequently E. lovingly 1.____
2. A. obedient B. elaborate C. disgust D. bearing E. ambasador 2.____
3. A. awkward B. charitable C. typhoid D. compitition E. ruffle 3.____
4. A. concervatory B. ninth C. morsel D. squirrels E. luxury 4.____
5. A. loyalty B. occasional C. hosiery D. bungalow E. undicided 5.____
6. A. efficient B. suberb C. achievement D. bored E. specimen 6.____
7. A. adaquate B. salaries C. utilize D. alcohol E. colonel 7.____
8. A. forcibly B. guardian C. preceeding D. quartile E. quizzes 8.____
9. A. seiges B. unanimous C. ridiculous D. everlasting E. omissions 9.____
10. A. itemized B. ignoramus C. adige D. adieu E. nickel 10.____
11. A. resources B. fileal C. nervous D. logical E. certificate 11.____
12. A. wiring B. turkeys C. morass D. obvious E. bigimmy 12.____
13. A. affirmitive B. noisy C. clothe D. carnage E. perceive 13.____
14. A. ignorant B. literally C. humerists D. business E. awkward 14.____
15. A. thermometer B. tragady C. partisan D. kinsman E. grandiose 15.____
16. A. fundamental B. herald C. delinquent D. kindergarden E. ascertain 16.____
17. A. apropriation B. year's C. vacancy D. enthusiastic E. dormitory 17.____
18. A. crochet B. courtesies C. troup D. occasionally E. spirits 18.____
19. A. typewriting B. inadequate C. legitimate D. fuelless E. restarant 19.____
20. A. tabloux B. cooperage C. wrapped D. tenant E. referring 20.____

KEY (CORRECT ANSWERS)

1. D. consequently
2. E. ambassador
3. D. competition
4. A. conservatory
5. E. undecided
6. B. suburb
7. A. adequate
8. C. preceding OR proceeding
9. A. sieges
10. C. adage
11. B. filial
12. E. bigamy
13. A. affirmative
14. C. humorists
15. B. tragedy
16. D. kindergarten
17. A. appropriation
18. C. troop OR troupe
19. E. restaurant
20. A. tableaux OR tableaus

TEST 2

DIRECTIONS: In each question of the following tests, select the letter of the one MISSPELLED word in each of the listed groups of five (5) words. *PRINT THE LETTER OF THE CORRECT ANSWER IN THE SPACE AT THE RIGHT.*

1. A. loot B. surgery C. breif D. talcum E. Christmas 1.____
2. A. commenced B. congenial C. fatal D. politician E. standerd 2.____
3. A. unbarable B. physician C. potato D. wiring E. adorable 3.____
4. A. error B. regretted C. instetute D. typhoid E. we're 4.____
5. A. merly B. opportunity C. patterns D. unctious E. righteous 5.____
6. A. luxury B. forty C. control D. originally E. intemate 6.____
7. A. plague B. ignorance C. poltrey D. hence E. bruise 7.____
8. A. athletic B. exebition C. leased D. interrupt E. spirits 8.____
9. A. destruction B. prairie C. quartet D. status E. competators 9.____
10. A. triumph B. utility C. loyalty D. antisapte E. crochet 10.____
11. A. lieutenant B. recrute C. thermometer D. quantities E. usefulness 11.____
12. A. wholly B. sitting C. probably D. criticism E. lynche 12.____
13. A. anteque B. galvanized C. mercantile D. academy E. defense 13.____
14. A. kinsman B. declaration C. absurd D. dispach E. patience 14.____
15. A. opportune B. abbuting C. warranted D. refrigerator E. raisin 15.____
16. A. deffered B. principalship C. lovable D. athletic E. conveniently 16.____
17. A. mislaid B. receipted C. skedule D. mission E. whereabouts 17.____
18. A. tuition B. unnatural C. remodel D. consequence E. misdameanor 18.____
19. A. assessment B. advises C. embassys D. border E. leased 19.____
20. A. morale B. legitemate C. infamy D. indebtedness E. technical 20.____

KEY (CORRECT ANSWERS)

1. C. brief
2. E. standard
3. A. unbearable
4. C. institute
5. A. merely
6. E. intimate
7. C. poultry OR paltry
8. B. exhibition
9. E. competition
10. D. anticipate
11. B. recruit
12. E. lynch
13. A. antique
14. D. dispatch
15. B. abutting
16. A. deferred OR differed
17. C. schedule
18. E. misdemeanor
19. C. embassies
20. B. legitimate

TEST 3

DIRECTIONS: In each question of the following tests, select the letter of the one MIS-SPELLED word in each of the listed groups of five (5) words. *PRINT THE LETTER OF THE CORRECT ANSWER IN THE SPACE AT THE RIGHT.*

1. A. stepfather B. fireman C. loot D. conclusivly E. commodity 1.____
2. A. mislaid B. roommate C. religous D. thesis E. temporary 2.____
3. A. statutes B. malice C. unbridled D. aisle E. cavelry 3.____
4. A. aknowledge B. immensely C. quantities D. erratic E. postponed 4.____
5. A. people's B. foreign C. obsticles D. opportunity E. cordially 5.____
6. A. fragrance B. burgaleries C. clothe D. twins E. herculean 6.____
7. A. warranted B. yoke C. democrat D. parashute E. Bible 7.____
8. A. existance B. enthusiasm C. medal D. sandwiches E. dunce 8.____
9. A. loyalty B. eternal C. chanceler D. psychology E. assessment 9.____
10. A. bungalow B. mutilate C. forcible D. ridiculous E. cawcus 10.____
11. A. lieutenant B. abandoned C. successor D. phisycal E. inquiries 11.____
12. A. nuisance B. coranation C. voluntary D. faculties E. awe 12.____
13. A. indipendance B. notwithstanding C. tariff D. opportune E. accompanying 13.____
14. A. statutes B. rhubarb C. corset D. prurient E. subsedy 14.____
15. A. partisan B. initiate C. colonel D. ilness E. errant 15.____
16. A. acquired B. wrapped C. propriater D. screech E. dune 16.____
17. A. sufrage B. countenance C. fraternally D. undo E. fireman 17.____
18. A. ladies B. chef C. spirituelist D. Sabbath E. itemized 18.____
19. A. ere B. interests C. cheesecloth D. paridoxical E. garish 19.____
20. A. bulletin B. neutral C. porttiere D. discretion E. inconvenienced 20.____

KEY (CORRECT ANSWERS)

1. D. conclusively
2. C. religious
3. E. cavalry
4. A. acknowledge
5. C. obstacles
6. B. burglaries
7. D. parachute
8. A. existence
9. C. chancellor
10. E. caucus
11. D. physical
12. B. coronation
13. A. independence
14. E. subsidy
15. D. illness
16. C. proprietor
17. A. suffrage
18. C. spiritualist
19. D. paradoxical
20. C. portiere

TEST 4

DIRECTIONS: In each question of the following tests, select the letter of the one MISSPELLED word in each of the listed groups of five (5) words. *PRINT THE LETTER OF THE CORRECT ANSWER IN THE SPACE AT THE RIGHT.*

1. A. I'd B. premises C. hysterics D. aparantly E. faculties 1.____
2. A. discipline B. ajurnment C. bachelor D. lose E. wrapped 2.____
3. A. simular B. bulletin C. lovable D. bored E. quizzes 3.____
4. A. attendance B. preparation C. refrigerator D. cafateria E. twelfth 4.____
5. A. inconvenienced B. courtesies C. raisin D. hosiery E. politicean 5.____
6. A. reccommendation B. colonel C. sandwiches D. women's E. undoubtedly 6.____
7. A. technical B. imediately C. temporarily D. dormitory E. voluntary 7.____
8. A. salaries B. abandoned C. consistent D. unconcious E. herald 8.____
9. A. duly B. leer C. emphasise D. vacant E. requisition 9.____
10. A. melancholy B. citrus C. omissions D. bazaar E. derigable 10.____
11. A. acquired B. mercury C. stetistics D. thought E. vassal 11.____
12. A. tempature B. calendar C. series D. gout E. alcohol 12.____
13. A. important B. foreigner C. Australia D. leggend E. rhythm 13.____
14. A. height B. achevement C. monarchial D. axle E. fertile 14.____
15. A. falsity B. prestige C. conquer D. arketecture E. Jerusalem 15.____
16. A. magnifecent B. bacteria C. holly D. diseases E. cellar 16.____
17. A. medicine B. grievous C. beaker D. benefits E. attendents 17.____
18. A. military B. vacancy C. weird D. feudalism E. hybird 18.____
19. A. adopted B. agrigate C. Renaissance D. tournament E. colonies 19.____
20. A. vivisection B. penitentiary C. candadacy D. seer E. Sabbath 20.____

KEY (CORRECT ANSWERS)

1. D. apparently
2. B. adjournment
3. A. similar
4. D. cafeteria
5. E. politician
6. A. recommendation
7. B. immediately
8. D. unconscious
9. C. emphasizes or emphasis
10. E. dirigible
11. C. statistics
12. A. temperature
13. D. legend
14. B. achievement
15. D. architecture
16. A. magnificent
17. E. attendants
18. E. hybrid
19. B. aggregate
20. C. candidacy

TEST 5

DIRECTIONS: In each question of the following tests, select the letter of the one MISSPELLED word in each of the listed groups of five (5) words. *PRINT THE LETTER OF THE CORRECT ANSWER IN THE SPACE AT THE RIGHT.*

1. A. acknowledging B. deligate C. foliage D. staid E. loot 1._____
2. A. gandar B. losing C. notwithstanding D. worlds E. torrent 2._____
3. A. medal B. utilize C. efficiency D. apricot E. soliceting 3._____
4. A. museum B. Christian C. possesion D. occasional E. bored 4._____
5. A. capitol B. sieze C. premises D. fragrance E. tonnage 5._____
6. A. requisition B. faculties C. canon D. chaufur E. stomach 6._____
7. A. solemn B. ascertain C. I'll D. chef E. delinquant 7._____
8. A. parliments B. distributor C. voluntary D. lovable E. counsel 8._____
9. A. morale B. democrat C. rhumatism D. dormitory E. leased 9._____
10. A. screech B. missapropriating C. courtesies D. wraith E. furlough 10._____
11. A. tryst B. tarriff C. visible D. accent E. contraries 11._____
12. A. dizzy B. leggings C. steak D. compaine E. interior 12._____
13. A. profit B. tiranny C. shocked D. response E. innocent 13._____
14. A. freshman B. vague C. larsiny D. ignorant E. worrying 14._____
15. A. disatesfied B. jealous C. unfortunately D. economical E. lettuce 15._____
16. A. based B. primarily C. condemned D. accompanied E. dupped 16._____
17. A. superntendant B. veil C. congenial D. quantities E. ere 17._____
18. A. unanimous B. dessert C. undoubtedly D. kolera E. nuisance 18._____
19. A. woman's B. bolero C. 'tis D. Pullman E. envellop 19._____
20. A. initiate B. grist C. pagent D. mention E. adieu 20._____

KEY (CORRECT ANSWERS)

1. B. delegate
2. A. gander
3. E. soliciting
4. C. possession
5. B. seize
6. D. chauffeur
7. E. delinquent
8. A. parliaments
9. C. rheumatism
10. B. misappropriating
11. B. tariff
12. D. campaign
13. B. tyranny
14. C. larceny
15. A. dissatisfied
16. E. duped
17. A. superintendent
18. D. cholera
19. E. envelope
20. C. pageant

TEST 6

DIRECTIONS: In each question of the following tests, select the letter of the one MISSPELLED word in each of the listed groups of five (5) words. *PRINT THE LETTER OF THE CORRECT ANSWER IN THE SPACE AT THE RIGHT.*

1. A. attach   B. voucher   C. twins   D. assistence   E. cordial   1.____
2. A. faculties   B. people's   C. indetedness   D. ignorant   E. resource   2.____
3. A. wholly   B. apitite   C. twelfth   D. unauthorized   E. embroider   3.____
4. A. certified   B. attorneys   C. foggy   D. potato   E. extravigent   4.____
5. A. hysterics   B. simelar   C. intelligent   D. label   E. salaries   5.____
6. A. apponants   B. we're   C. finely   D. herald   E. continuous   6.____
7. A. cancellation   B. athletic   C. perminant   D. preference   E. utilize   7.____
8. A. urns   B. zephyr   C. tuition   D. incidentally   E. aquisition   8.____
9. A. kinsaan   B. bazaar   C. foliage   D. wretched   E. asassination   9.____
10. A. insignia   B. bimonthly   C. typewriting   D. notariety   E. psychology   10.____
11. A. continually   B. guild   C. vegtable   D. vague   E. patience   11.____
12. A. desease   B. parole   C. gallery   D. awkward   E. you'd   12.____
13. A. border   B. warrant   C. operated   D. economics   E. ilegal   13.____
14. A. fatal   B. agatation   C. obliged   D. studying   E. resignation   14.____
15. A. ammendment   B. promptness   C. glimpse   D. canon   E. tract   15.____
16. A. wholly   B. apricot   C. destruction   D. pappal   E. leisure   16.____
17. A. issuing   B. rabbid   C. unusual   D. parasite   E. khaki   17.____
18. A. nowadays   B. courtesies   C. negotiate   D. gaurdian   E. derrick   18.____
19. A. partisan   B. seanse   C. vacancy   D. fragrance   E. corps   19.____
20. A. equipped   B. nuisance   C. phrenology   D. foriegn   E. insignia   20.____

KEY (CORRECT ANSWERS)

1. D. assistance
2. C. indebtedness
3. B. appetite
4. E. extravagant
5. B. similar
6. A. opponents
7. C. permanent
8. E. acquisition
9. E. assassination
10. D. notoriety
11. C. vegetable
12. A. disease
13. E. illegal
14. B. agitation
15. A. amendment
16. D. papal
17. B. rabid
18. D. guardian
19. B. eance
20. D. foreign

———

TEST 7

DIRECTIONS: In each question of the following tests, select the letter of the one MIS-SPELLED word in each of the listed groups of five (5) words. *PRINT THE LETTER OF THE CORRECT ANSWER IN THE SPACE AT THE RIGHT.*

1. A. frightfully B. mantain C. post office D. specific E. bachelor 1._____
2. A. cease B. turkeys C. woman's D. hustling E. weild 2._____
3. A. expidition B. valuing C. typhoid D. grapevines E. advice 3._____
4. A. balance B. visible C. correspondant D. etc. E. arctic 4._____
5. A. benefit B. arkives C. classified D. inasmuch E. sincerity 5._____
6. A. obedient B. vengeance C. plague D. fascinate E. contageous 6._____
7. A. desicion B. partner C. economy D. piece E. arrogant 7._____
8. A. dyeing B. lightning C. millenary D. undulate E. embarrass 8._____
9. A. strenuous B. isicle C. panel D. suburb E. luxury 9._____
10. A. aisle B. proffer C. people's D. condemed E. morale 10._____
11. A. advising B. recognizing C. seize D. supply E. tradegy 11._____
12. A. intensive B. stationary C. benifit D. equipped E. preferring 12._____
13. A. predjudice B. pervade C. excel D. capitol E. chimera 13._____
14. A. all right B. ninty C. cronies D. nervous E. separate 14._____
15. A. atheletic B. queue C. schedule D. furl E. credible 15._____
16. A. inevitable B. sincerly C. monkeys D. definite E. cynical 16._____
17. A. niece B. accommodate C. loveliness D. reciept E. forcibly 17._____
18. A. cancel B. chagrined C. allies D. playwright E. liutenant 18._____
19. A. pageant B. alcohol C. villian D. Odyssey E. criticize 19._____
20. A. acknowledge B. article C. contemptible D. taciturn E. sovreign 20._____

KEY (CORRECT ANSWERS)

1. B. maintain
2. E. wield
3. A. expedition
4. C. correspondent
5. B. archives
6. E. contagious
7. A. decision
8. C. millinery
9. B. icicle
10. D. condemned
11. E. tragedy
12. C. benefit
13. A. prejudice
14. B. ninety
15. A. athletic
16. B. sincerely
17. D. receipt
18. E. lieutenant
19. C. villain
20. E. sovereign

TEST 8

DIRECTIONS: In each question of the following tests, select the letter of the one MISSPELLED word in each of the listed groups of five (5) words. *PRINT THE LETTER OF THE CORRECT ANSWER IN THE SPACE AT THE RIGHT.*

1. A. incurred   B. cieling   C. strengthen   D. carnage   E. typical   1.____
2. A. twins   B. year's   C. acutely   D. changible   E. facility   2.____
3. A. deliscious B. enormous   C. likeness   D. witnesses   E. commodity   3.____
4. A. scenes   B. enlargement C. discretion   D. acknowledging   E. sesion   4.____
5. A. annum   B. strenuous   C. tretchery   D. infamy   E. opportune   5.____
6. A. marmelade B. loot   C. kinsman   D. crochet   E. hawser   6.____
7. A. sophmore   B. duly   C. across   D. lovable   E. propaganda   7.____
8. A. quantities B. rickety   C. roommate   D. penetentiary   E. lose   8.____
9. A. interrupt B. cauldron   C. convienient D. successor   E. apiece   9.____
10. A. acquire   B. incesent   C. forfeit   D. typewritten   E. dysentery   10.____
11. A. inferred B. whisle   C. jovial   D. conscript   E. gracious   11.____
12. A. tantalizing B. ominous   C. conductor   D. duchess   E. telegram   12.____
13. A. reconcile B. primitive   C. sausy   D. quinine   E. cede   13.____
14. A. immagine B. viaduct   C. chisel   D. Saturn   E. currant   14.____
15. A. amplify   B. greace   C. cholera   D. perilous   E. theology   15.____
16. A. pursevere B. deodorize   C. ligament   D. illuminate   E. dropsy   16.____
17. A. cavalier B. transparent C. perjury   D. vicinaty   E. navigate   17.____
18. A. postpone B. dictaphone   C. corral   D. alligator   E. arteficial   18.____
19. A. cannon   B. hospital   C. distilliry   D. righteous   E. secession   19.____
20. A. matrimony B. digestable   C. scrutiny   D. artisan   E. mediocre   20.____

KEY (CORRECT ANSWERS)

1. B. ceiling
2. D. changeable
3. A. delicious
4. E. session
5. C. treachery
6. A. marmalade
7. A. sophomore
8. D. penitentiary
9. C. convenient
10. B. incessant
11. B. whistle
12. E. telegram
13. C. saucy
14. A. imagine
15. B. grease
16. A. persevere
17. D. vicinity
18. E. artificial
19. C. distillery
20. B. digestible

TEST 9

DIRECTIONS: In each question of the following tests, select the letter of the one MISSPELLED word in each of the listed groups of five (5) words. *PRINT THE LETTER OF THE CORRECT ANSWER IN THE SPACE AT THE RIGHT.*

1. A. feirce B. ascent C. allies D. doctor E. coming 1.____
2. A. hopeless B. absense C. foretell D. certain E. similar 2.____
3. A. advise B. muscle C. manual D. provocation E. copywright 3.____
4. A. behooves B. reservoir C. frostbiten D. squalor E. ambuscade 4.____
5. A. systematic B. precious C. tremendos D. insulation E. brilliant 5.____
6. A. significant B. jurisdiction C. libel D. monkies E. legacy 6.____
7. A. dual B. authentic C. serenety D. mechanism E. suburban 7.____
8. A. candel B. dissolution C. laceration D. portend E. pigeon 8.____
9. A. loyalty B. periodic C. presume D. led E. suprano 9.____
10. A. mania B. medicinal C. dungarees D. overwelming E. masquerade 10.____
11. A. pitiful B. latter C. ommitted D. agreement E. reconcile 11.____
12. A. bananna B. routine C. likewise D. indecent E. habitually 12.____
13. A. relieve B. copys C. ninety D. crowded E. electoral 13.____
14. A. adviseable B. illustrative C. financial D. nevertheless E. chimneys 14.____
15. A. prisioner B. immediate C. statistics D. surgeon E. abscond 15.____
16. A. option B. extradite C. comparitive D. jealousy E. illusion 16.____
17. A. handicaped B. assurance C. sympathy D. speech E. dining 17.____
18. A. recommend B. carraige C. disapprove D. independent E. mortgage 18.____
19. A. systematic B. ingenuity C. tenet D. uncanny E. intrigueing 19.____
20. A. arduous B. hideous C. fervant D. companies E. breach 20.____

KEY (CORRECT ANSWERS)

1. A. fierce
2. B. absence
3. E. copyright
4. C. frostbitten
5. C. tremendous
6. D. monkeys
7. C. serenity
8. A. candle
9. E. soprano
10. D. overwhelming
11. C. omitted
12. A. banana
13. B. copies
14. A. advisable
15. A. prisoner
16. C. comparative
17. A. handicapped
18. B. carriage
19. E. intriguing
20. C. fervent

TEST 10

DIRECTIONS: In each question of the following tests, select the letter of the one MIS-SPELLED word in each of the listed groups of five (5) words. *PRINT THE LETTER OF THE CORRECT ANSWER IN THE SPACE AT THE RIGHT.*

1. A. together B. attempt C. loyality D. innocent E. rinse 1.____
2. A. argueing B. emergency C. kindergarten D. religious E. schedule 2.____
3. A. society B. anticipate C. dissatisfy D. responsable E. temporary 3.____
4. A. chaufeur B. grammar C. planned D. dining room E. accurate 4.____
5. A. confidence B. maturity C. aspirations D. evasion E. insurance 5.____
6. A. unnecessary B. dirigible C. transparant D. similar E. appetite 6.____
7. A. treachery B. comedian C. arrest D. recollect E. mistep 7.____
8. A. falsify B. blight C. flexible D. drasticaly E. meddlesome 8.____
9. A. congestion B. publickly C. receipts D. academic E. paralyze 9.____
10. A. possibilities B. undergoes C. consistant D. aggression E. pledge 10.____
11. A. wrist B. welfare C. necessity D. scenery E. tendancy 11.____
12. A. commiting B. accusation C. endurance D. agreeable E. excitable 12.____
13. A. despair B. surgury C. privilege D. appreciation E. journeying 13.____
14. A. cameos B. propaganda C. delicious D. heathen E. interupt 14.____
15. A. relieve B. disappear C. development D. matress E. ninety-nine 15.____
16. A. finally B. bullitin C. doctor D. desirable E. sincerely 16.____
17. A. wrest B. array C. auspices D. sacrafice E. generations 17.____
18. A. liquid B. vegetable C. silence D. familiar E. fasinate 18.____
19. A. tomato B. suspence C. leisure D. license E. permanent 19.____
20. A. characteristic B. soliciting C. repitious D. immediately E. extravagant 20.____

KEY (CORRECT ANSWERS)

1. C. loyalty
2. A. arguing
3. D. responsible
4. A. chauffeur
5. E. insurance
6. C. transparent
7. E. misstep
8. D. drastically
9. B. publicly
10. C. consistent
11. E. tendency
12. A. committing
13. B. surgery
14. E. interrupt
15. D. mattress
16. B. bulletin
17. D. sacrifice
18. E. fascinate
19. B. suspense
20. C. repetitious

SPELLING
EXAMINATION SECTION
TEST 1

DIRECTIONS: One word in each lettered group is misspelled. Indicate the letter of the misspelled word in the space at the right. Mark "E" if all are spelled correctly.

1.	A. sacriligious	B. ingenius	C. advantageous	D. ingenuous	1.____
2.	A. apparrel	B. barrel	C. quarrel	D. sorrel	2.____
3.	A. carousal	B. cannester	C. carrousel	D. cygnet	3.____
4.	A. preliminary	B. cemetary	C. seminary	D. eleemosynary	4.____
5.	A. croquet	B. kimono	C. cocoanut	D. carom	5.____
6.	A. chattel	B. privelege	C. convenience	D. immerse	6.____
7.	A. resiliant	B. aspirant	C. adherent	D. conversant	7.____
8.	A. sacrilege	B. entourage	C. demurage	D. persiflage	8.____
9.	A. disappoint	B. dissatisfy	C. dessicate	D. dissuade	9.____
10.	A. fallacy	B. fantasy	C. ecstacy	D. hypocrisy	10.____
11.	A. elegible	B. illegible	C. intelligible	D. irascible	11.____
12.	A. emission	B. omission	C. incision	D. comission	12.____
13.	A. narrate	B. exaggerrate	C. disintegrate	D. hyphenate	13.____
14.	A. chagrined	B. humbugged	C. kidnapped	D. fidgetted	14.____
15.	A. flaccid	B. succinct	C. rancid	D. accrid	15.____
16.	A. forehead	B. foresworn	C. foresight	D. forerunner	16.____
17.	A. guard	B. language	C. guarantee	D. guage	17.____
18.	A. embarrassed	B. harrassed	C. terraced	D. harnessed	18.____
19.	A. persuade	B. imperterbable	C. pursuit	D. purport	19.____
20.	A. innuendo	B. inoculate	C. inovation	D. innocuous	20.____
21.	A. weird	B. inviegle	C. siege	D. seized	21.____
22.	A. ratify	B. rarefy	C. liquify	D. ramify	22.____
23.	A. muscles	B. mussels	C. missals	D. missies	23.____
24.	A. Philippines	B. penicillen	C. patrolling	D. prairie	24.____
25.	A. questionaire	B. fanfare	C. flair	D. solitaire	25.____

KEY (CORRECT ANSWERS)

1.	A	sacrilegious
2.	A	apparel
3.	B	cannister
4.	B	cemetery
5.	E	
6.	B	privilege
7.	A	resilient
8.	C	demurrage
9.	C	desiccate
10.	C	ecstasy
11.	A	eligible
12.	D	commission
13.	B	exaggerate
14.	D	fidgeted
15.	D	acrid
16.	B	forsworn
17.	D	gauge
18.	B	harassed
19.	B	imperturbable
20.	C	innovation
21.	B	inveigle
22.	C	liquefy
23.	D	missiles
24.	B	penicillin
25.	A	questionnaire

TEST 2

DIRECTIONS: Two words in each lettered group are INCORRECTLY spelled. Indicate the two misspelled words in each group in the space at the right.

1. A. accidently   B. apology   C. description   D. devide   1._____
2. A. accomodate   B. apparatus   C. business   D. desireable   2._____
3. A. arguement   B. conscience   C. dining   D. convience   3._____
4. A. across   B. atheletics   C. changeable   D. dissapoint   4._____
5. A. choose   B. disasterous   C. dissatisfied D. courtecy   5._____
6. A. all right   B. allready   C. almost   D. alltogether   6._____
7. A. eighth   B. formerly   C. formaly   D. begining   7._____
8. A. ninth   B. forty   C. embarrasment D. ninty   8._____
9. A. fourth   B. lose   C. noticable   D. enviroment   9._____
10. A. grammer   B. irrelevent   C. weight   D. either   10._____
11. A. familar   B. similiar   C. its   D. width   11._____
12. A. occassionally B. occurence   C. government   D. exceed   12._____
13. A. labatory   B. necessary   C. outragous   D. paid   13._____
14. A. dipthong   B. pamphlett   C. hoping   D. illegible   14._____
15. A. beleive   B. concieve   C. quite   D. quiet   15._____
16. A. benefited   B. preferable   C. wheather   D. grievious   16._____
17. A. counterfeit B. serviceable   C. conferance   D. confidentally   17._____
18. A. quantity   B. quality   C. probally   D. libary   18._____
19. A. recieve   B. decieve   C. perform   D. preferred   19._____
20. A. reconize   B. seperate   C. truly   D. inter   20._____
21. A. perfessor   B. useing   C. proceed   D. impede   21._____
22. A. you're   B. it's   C. preceed   D. impeed   22._____
23. A. possession   B. pursue   C. pursuade   D. religeous   23._____
24. A. rhythm   B. schedule   C. repitition   D. usualy   24._____
25. A. mileage   B. peaceable   C. minature   D. superintendant 25._____

KEY (CORRECT ANSWERS)

1.	A,D	accidentally, divide
2.	A,D	accommodate, desirable
3.	A,D	argument, convenience
4.	A,D	athletics, disappoint
5.	B,D	disastrous, courtesy
6.	B,D	already, altogether
7.	C,D	formally, beginning
8.	C,D	embarrassment, ninety
9.	C,D	noticeable, environment
10.	A,B	grammar, irrelevant
11.	A,B	familiar, similar
12.	A,B	occasionally, occurrence
13.	A,C	laboratory, outrageous
14.	A,B	diphthong, pamphlet
15.	A,B	believe, conceive
16.	C,D	whether, grievous
17.	C,D	conference, confidentially
18.	C,D	probably, library
19.	A,B	receive, deceive
20.	A,B	recognize, separate
21.	A,B	professor, using
22.	C,D	precede, impede
23.	C,D	persuade, religious
24.	C,D	repetition, usually
25.	C,D	miniature, superintendent

TEST 3

DIRECTIONS: Two words in each lettered group are INCORRECTLY spelled. Indicate the two misspelled words in each group in the space at the right.

1. A. consolible   B. libel   C. inteligible   D. irascible   1.____
2. A. beneficient   B. correlative   C. awful   D. offeng   2.____
3. A. tractible   B. malleable   C. tracable   D. exchangeable   3.____
4. A. inviegle   B. weird   C. seige   D. seized   4.____
5. A. recommend   B. saccharine   C. dillemma   D. millenium   5.____
6. A. dissipated   B. loneliness   C. incidently   D. corroberate   6.____
7. A. advantageous B. ingenious   C. facetous   D. ingenous   7.____
8. A. inoculate   B. innuendo   C. inovation   D. inocuous   8.____
9. A. embarassed   B. harrassed   C. harnessed   D. terraced   9.____
10. A. monsignier   B. mayorality   C. saxophone   D. liquefied   10.____
11. A. caravansery B. compulsary   C. anniversary   D. adversary   11.____
12. A. duteable   B. scurilous   C. beseech   D. catechized   12.____
13. A. exaggerate   B. narrate   C. disintigrate   D. hyphenate   13.____
14. A. ommission   B. emission   C. omnitient   D. commission   14.____
15. A. persuit   B. purser   C. imperterbable   D. purport   15.____
16. A. adherrent   B. conversant   C. resiliant   D. aspirant   16.____
17. A. mussels   B. missils   C. missles   D. muscles   17.____
18. A. palaver   B. deffer   C. profer   D. prefer   18.____
19. A. million   B. batallion   C. pavillion   D. stallion   19.____
20. A. inability   B. intelligibility C. elligibility   D. fallability   20.____
21. A. alottment   B. equipment   C. detrement   D. installment   21.____
22. A. foresworn   B. forehead   C. forsight   D. forerunner   22.____
23. A. guage   B. language   C. gaurantee   D. guard   23.____
24. A. sorel   B. apparrel   C. barrel   D. quarrel   24.____
25. A. questionaire B. flaire   C. fanfare   D. solitary   25.____

KEY (CORRECT ANSWERS)

1.	A,C	consolable, intelligible
2.	A,D	beneficent, offing
3.	A,C	tractable, traceable
4.	A,C	inveigle, siege
5.	C,D	dilemma, millennium
6.	C,D	incidentally, corroborate
7.	C,D	facetious, ingenious
8.	C,D	innovation, innocuous
9.	A,B	embarrassed, harassed
10.	A,B	monsignior, mayoralty
11.	A,B	caravansary, compulsory
12.	A,B	dutiable, scurrilous
13.	A,C	exaggerate, disintegrate
14.	A,C	omission, omniscient
15.	A,C	pursuit, imperturbable
16.	A,C	adherent, resilient
17.	B,C	missals, missiles
18.	B,C	defer, proffer
19.	B,C	battalion, pavilion
20.	C,D	eligibility, fallibility
21.	A,C	allotment, detriment
22.	A,C	forsworn, foresight
23.	A,C	gauge, guarantee
24.	A,B	sorrel, apparel
25.	A,B	questionnaire, flair

SPELLING

EXAMINATION SECTION

TEST 1

DIRECTIONS: In each of the following tests in this part, select the letter of the one MISSPELLED word in each of the following groups of words. *PRINT THE LETTER OF THE CORRECT ANSWER IN THE SPACE AT THE RIGHT.*

1. A. grateful   B. fundimental   C. census   D. analysis   1.____
2. A. installment   B. retrieve   C. concede   D. dissapear   2.____
3. A. accidentaly   B. dismissal   C. conscientious D. indelible   3.____
4. A. perceive   B. carreer   C. anticipate   D. acquire   4.____
5. A. facillity   B. reimburse   C. assortment   D. guidance   5.____
6. A. plentiful   B. across   C. advantagous   D. similar   6.____
7. A. omission   B. pamphlet   C. guarrantee   D. repel   7.____
8. A. maintenance   B. always   C. liable   D. anouncement   8.____
9. A. exaggerate   B. sieze   C. condemn   D. commit   9.____
10. A. pospone   B. altogether   C. grievance   D. excessive   10.____
11. A. banana   B. trafic   C. spectacle   D. boundary   11.____
12. A. commentator B. abbreviation C. battaries   D. monastery   12.____
13. A. practically B. advise   C. pursuade   D. laboratory   13.____
14. A. fatigueing   B. invincible   C. strenuous   D. ceiling   14.____
15. A. propeller   B. reverence   C. piecemeal   D. underneth   15.____
16. A. annonymous   B. envelope   C. transit   D. variable   16.____
17. A. petroleum   B. bigoted   C. meager   D. resistence   17.____

2 (#1)

18. A. permissible   B. indictment   C. fundemental   D. nowadays   18.____
19. A. thief   B. bargin   C. nuisance   D. vacant   19.____
20. A. technique   B. vengeance   C. aquatic   D. heighth   20.____

KEY (CORRECT ANSWERS)

1. B. fundamental
2. D. disappear
3. A. accidentally
4. B. career
5. A. facility

6. C. advantageous
7. C. guarantee
8. D. announcement
9. B. seize
10. A. postpone

11. B. traffic
12. C. batteries
13. C. persuade
14. A. fatiguing
15. D. underneath

16. A. anonymous
17. D. resistance
18. C. fundamental
19. B. bargain
20. D. height

TEST 2

DIRECTIONS: In each of the following tests in this part, select the letter of the one MISSPELLED word in each of the following groups of words. *PRINT THE LETTER OF THE CORRECT ANSWER IN THE SPACE AT THE RIGHT.*

1. A. apparent B. superintendent C. relieve D. calendar 1.____
2. A. foreign B. negotiate C. typical D. disipline 2.____
3. A. posponed B. argument C. susceptible D. deficit 3.____
4. A. preferred B. column C. peculiar D. equiped 4.____
5. A. exaggerate B. disatisfied C. repetition D. already 5.____
6. A. livelihood B. physician C. obsticle D. strategy 6.____
7. A. courageous B. ommission C. ridiculous D. awkward 7.____
8. A. sincerely B. abundance C. negligable D. elementary 8.____
9. A. obsolete B. mischievous C. enumerate D. atheletic 9.____
10. A. fiscel B. beneficiary C. concede D. translate 10.____
11. A. segregate B. excessivly C. territory D. obstacle 11.____
12. A. unnecessary B. monopolys C. harmonious D. privilege 12.____
13. A. sinthetic B. intellectual C. gracious D. archaic 13.____
14. A. beneficial B. fulfill C. sarcastic D. disolve 14.____
15. A. umbrella B. sentimental C. inefficent D. psychiatrist 15.____
16. A. noticable B. knapsack C. librarian D. meant 16.____
17. A. conference B. upheaval C. vulger D. odor 17.____
18. A. surmount B. pentagon C. calorie D. inumerable 18.____
19. A. classifiable B. moisturize C. monitor D. assesment 19.____
20. A. thermastat B. corrupting C. approach D. thinness 20.____

KEY (CORRECT ANSWERS)

1. C. relieve
2. D. discipline
3. A. postponed
4. D. equipped
5. B. dissatisfied

6. C. obstacle
7. B. omission
8. C. negligible
9. D. athletic
10. A. fiscal

11. B. excessively
12. B. monopolies
13. A. synthetic
14. D. dissolve
15. C. inefficient

16. A. noticeable
17. C. vulgar
18. D. innumerable
19. D. assessment
20. A. thermostat

TEST 3

DIRECTIONS: In each of the following tests in this part, select the letter of the one MISSPELLED word in each of the following groups of words. *PRINT THE LETTER OF THE CORRECT ANSWER IN THE SPACE AT THE RIGHT.*

1. A. typical   B. descend   C. summarize   D. continuel   1.____
2. A. courageous   B. recomend   C. omission   D. eliminate   2.____
3. A. compliment   B. illuminate   C. auxilary   D. installation   3.____
4. A. preliminary   B. aquainted   C. syllable   D. analysis   4.____
5. A. accustomed   B. negligible   C. interupted   D. bulletin   5.____
6. A. summoned   B. managment   C. mechanism   D. sequence   6.____
7. A. commitee   B. surprise   C. noticeable   D. emphasize   7.____
8. A. occurrance   B. likely   C. accumulate   D. grievance   8.____
9. A. obstacle   B. particuliar   C. baggage   D. fascinating   9.____
10. A. innumerable   B. seize   C. applicant   D. dictionery   10.____
11. A. monkeys   B. rigid   C. unnatural   D. roomate   11.____
12. A. surveying   B. figurative   C. famous   D. curiosety   12.____
13. A. rodeo   B. inconcievable   C. calendar   D. magnificence   13.____
14. A. handicaped   B. glacier   C. defiance   D. emperor   14.____
15. A. schedule   B. scrawl   C. seclusion   D. sissors   15.____
16. A. tissues   B. tomatos   C. tyrants   D. tragedies   16.____
17. A. casette   B. graceful   C. penicillin   D. probably   17.____
18. A. gnawed   B. microphone   C. clinicle   D. batch   18.____
19. A. amateur   B. altitude   C. laborer   D. expence   19.____
20. A. mandate   B. flexable   C. despise   D. verify   20.____

KEY (CORRECT ANSWERS)

1. D. continual
2. B. recommend
3. C. auxiliary
4. B. acquainted
5. C. interrupted

6. B. management
7. A. committee
8. A. occurrence
9. B. particular
10. D. dictionary

11. D. roommate
12. D. curiosity
13. B. inconceivable
14. A. handicapped
15. D. scissors

16. B. tomatoes
17. A. cassette
18. C. clinical
19. D. expense
20. B. flexible

TEST 4

DIRECTIONS: In each of the following tests in this part, select the letter of the one MISSPELLED word in each of the following groups of words. *PRINT THE LETTER OF THE CORRECT ANSWER IN THE SPACE AT THE RIGHT.*

1. A. primery B. mechanic C. referred D. admissible 1._____
2. A. cessation B. beleif C. aggressive D. allowance 2._____
3. A. leisure B. authentic C. familiar D. contemtable 3._____
4. A. volume B. forty C. dilemma D. seldum 4._____
5. A. discrepancy B. aquisition C. exorbitant D. lenient 5._____
6. A. simultanous B. penetrate C. revision D. conspicuous 6._____
7. A. ilegible B. gracious C. profitable D. obedience 7._____
8. A. manufacturer B. authorize C. compelling D. pecular 8._____
9. A. anxious B. rehearsal C. handicaped D. tendency 9._____
10. A. meticulous B. accompaning C. initiative D. shelves 10._____
11. A. hammaring B. insecticide C. capacity D. illogical 11._____
12. A. budget B. luminous C. aviation D. lunchon 12._____
13. A. moniter B. bachelor C. pleasurable D. omitted 13._____
14. A. monstrous B. transistor C. narrative D. anziety 14._____
15. A. engagement B. judical C. pasteurize D. tried 15._____
16. A. fundimental B. innovation C. perpendicular D. extravagant 16._____
17. A. bookkeeper B. brutality C. gymnaseum D. cemetery 17._____
18. A. sturdily B. pretentious C. gourmet D. enterance 18._____
19. A. resturant B. tyranny C. kindergarten D. ancestry 19._____
20. A. benefit B. possess C. speciman D. noticing 20._____

KEY (CORRECT ANSWERS)

1. A. primary
2. B. belief
3. D. contemptible
4. D. seldom
5. B. acquisition

6. A. simultaneous
7. A. illegible
8. D. peculiar
9. C. handicapped
10. B. accompanying

11. A. hammering
12. D. luncheon
13. A. monitor
14. D. anxiety
15. B. judicial

16. A. fundamental
17. C. gymnasium
18. D. entrance
19. A. restaurant
20. C. specimen

TEST 5

DIRECTIONS: In each of the following tests in this part, select the letter of the one MISSPELLED word in each of the following groups of words. *PRINT THE LETTER OF THE CORRECT ANSWER IN THE SPACE AT THE RIGHT.*

1. A. arguing   B. correspondance   C. forfeit   D. dissension   1.____
2. A. occasion   B. description   C. prejudice   D. elegible   2.____
3. A. accomodate   B. initiative   C. changeable   D. enroll   3.____
4. A. temporary   B. insistent   C. benificial   D. separate   4.____
5. A. achieve   B. dissappoint   C. unanimous   D. judgment   5.____
6. A. procede   B. publicly   C. sincerity   D. successful   6.____
7. A. deceive   B. goverment   C. preferable   D. repetitive   7.____
8. A. emphasis   B. skillful   C. advisible   D. optimistic   8.____
9. A. tendency   B. rescind   C. crucial   D. noticable   9.____
10. A. privelege   B. abbreviate   C. simplify   D. divisible   10.____
11. A. irresistible   B. varius   C. mutual   D. refrigerator   11.____
12. A. amateur   B. distinguish   C. rehearsal   D. poision   12.____
13. A. biased   B. ommission   C. precious   D. coordinate   13.____
14. A. calculated   B. enthusiasm   C. sincerely   D. parashute   14.____
15. A. sentry   B. materials   C. incredable   D. budget   15.____
16. A. chocolate   B. instrument   C. volcanoe   D. shoulder   16.____
17. A. ancestry   B. obscure   C. intention   D. ninty   17.____
18. A. artical   B. bracelet   C. beggar   D. hopeful   18.____
19. A. tournament   B. sponsor   C. perpendiclar   D. dissolve   19.____
20. A. yeild   B. physician   C. greasiest   D. admitting   20.____

KEY (CORRECT ANSWERS)

1. B. correspondence
2. D. eligible
3. A. accommodate
4. C. beneficial
5. B. disappoint

6. A. proceed
7. B. government
8. C. advisable
9. D. noticeable
10. A. privilege

11. B. various
12. D. poison
13. B. omission
14. D. parachute
15. C. incredible

16. C. volcano
17. D. ninety
18. A. article
19. C. perpendicular
20. A. yield

TEST 6

DIRECTIONS: In each of the following tests in this part, select the letter of the one MISSPELLED word in each of the following groups of words. *PRINT THE LETTER OF THE CORRECT ANSWER IN THE SPACE AT THE RIGHT.*

1. A. achievment   B. maintenance   C. questionnaire   D. all are correct   1.____
2. A. prevelant   B. pronunciation C. separate   D. all are correct   2.____
3. A. permissible   B. relevant   C. seize   D. all are correct   3.____
4. A. corroborate   B. desparate   C. eighth   D. all are correct   4.____
5. A. exceed   B. feasibility   C. psycological   D. all are correct   5.____
6. A. parallel   B. aluminum   C. calendar   D. eigty   6.____
7. A. microbe   B. ancient   C. autograph   D. existance   7.____
8. A. plentiful   B. skillful   C. amoung   D. capsule   8.____
9. A. erupt   B. quanity   C. opinion   D. competent   9.____
10. A. excitement   B. discipline   C. luncheon   D. regreting   10.____
11. A. magazine   B. expository   C. imitation   D. permenent   11.____
12. A. ferosious   B. machinery   C. precise   D. magnificent   12.____
13. A. conceive   B. narritive   C. separation   D. management   13.____
14. A. muscular   B. witholding   C. pickle   D. glacier   14.____
15. A. vehicel   B. mismanage   C. correspondence D. dissatisfy   15.____
16. A. sentince   B. bulletin   C. notice   D. definition   16.____
17. A. appointment   B. exactly   C. typest   D. light   17.____
18. A. penalty   B. suparvise   C. consider   D. division   18.____
19. A. schedule   B. accurate   C. corect   D. simple   19.____
20. A. suggestion   B. installed   C. proper   D. agincy   20.____

KEY (CORRECT ANSWERS)

1. A. achievement
2. B. prevalent
3. D. all are correct
4. B. desperate
5. C. psychological

6. D. eighty
7. D. existence
8. C. among
9. B. quantity
10. D. regretting

11. D. permanent
12. A. ferocious
13. B. narrative
14. B. withholding
15. A. vehicle

16. A. sentence
17. C. typist
18. B. supervise
19. C. correct
20. D. agency

TEST 7

DIRECTIONS: In each of the following tests in this part, select the letter of the one MISSPELLED word in each of the following groups of words. *PRINT THE LETTER OF THE CORRECT ANSWER IN THE SPACE AT THE RIGHT.*

1. A. symtom   B. serum   B. antiseptic   D. aromatic   1.____
2. A. register   B. registrar   C. purser   D. burser   2.____
3. A. athletic   B. tragedy   C. batallion   D. sophomore   3.____
4. A. latent   B. godess   C. aisle   D. whose   4.____
5. A. rhyme   B. rhythm   C. thime   D. thine   5.____
6. A. eighth   B. exaggerate   C. electorial   D. villain   6.____
7. A. statute   B. superintendent   7.____
   C. iresistible   D. colleague
8. A. sieze   B. therefor   C. auxiliary   D. changeable   8.____
9. A. siege   B. knowledge   C. lieutenent   D. weird   9.____
10. A. acquitted   B. polititian   C. professor   D. conqueror   10.____
11. A. changeable   B. chargeable   C. salable   D. useable   11.____
12. A. promissory   B. prisoner   C. excellent   D. tyrrany   12.____
13. A. conspicuous   B. essance   C. comparative   D. brilliant   13.____
14. A. notefying   B. accentuate   C. adhesive   D. primarily   14.____
15. A. exercise   B. sublime   C. stuborn   D. shameful   15.____
16. A. presume   B. transcript   C. strech   D. wizard   16.____
17. A. specify   B. regional   C. arbitrary   D. segragation   17.____
18. A. requirement   B. happiness   C. achievement   D. gently   18.____
19. A. endurance   B. fusion   C. balloon   D. enormus   19.____
20. A. luckily   B. schedule   C. simplicity   D. sanwich   20.____

KEY (CORRECT ANSWERS)

1. A. symptom
2. D. bursar
3. C. battalion
4. B. goddess
5. C. thyme

6. C. electoral
7. C. irresistible
8. A. seize
9. C. lieutenant
10. B. politician

11. D. usable
12. D. tyranny
13. B. essence
14. A. notifying
15. C. stubborn

16. C. stretch
17. D. segregation
18. D. gently
19. D. enormous
20. D. sandwich

TEST 8

DIRECTIONS: In each of the following tests in this part, select the letter of the one MISSPELLED word in each of the following groups of words. *PRINT THE LETTER OF THE CORRECT ANSWER IN THE SPACE AT THE RIGHT.*

1. A. maintain B. maintainance C. sustain D. sustenance 1.____
2. A. portend B. portentious C. pretend D. pretentious 2.____
3. A. prophesize B. prophesies C. farinaceous D. spaceous 3.____
4. A. choose B. chose C. choosen D. chasten 4.____
5. A. censure B. censorious C. pleasure D. pleasurable 5.____
6. A. cover B. coverage C. adder D. adage 6.____
7. A. balloon B. diregible C. direct D. descent 7.____
8. A. whemsy B. crazy C. flimsy D. lazy 8.____
9. A. derision B. pretention C. sustention D. contention 9.____
10. A. question B. questionaire C. legion D. legionary 10.____
11. A. chattle B. cattle C. dismantle D. kindle 11.____
12. A. canal B. cannel C. chanel D. colonel 12.____
13. A. hemorrage B. storage C. manage D. foliage 13.____
14. A. surgeon B. sturgeon C. luncheon D. stancheon 14.____
15. A. diploma B. commission C. dependent D. luminious 15.____
16. A. likelihood B. blizzard C. machanical D. suppress 16.____
17. A. commercial B. releif C. disposal D. endeavor 17.____
18. A. operate B. bronco C. excaping D. grammar 18.____
19. A. orchard B. collar C. embarass D. distant 19.____
20. A. sincerly B. possessive C. weighed D. waist 20.____

KEY (CORRECT ANSWERS)

1. B. maintenance
2. B. portentous
3. D. spacious
4. C. chosen
5. D. pleasurable

6. D. adage
7. B. dirigible
8. A. whimsy
9. B. pretension
10. B. questionnaire

11. A. chattel
12. C. channel
13. A. hemorrhage
14. D. stanchion
15. D. luminous

16. C. mechanical
17. B. relief
18. C. escaping
19. C. embarrass
20. A. sincerely

———

TEST 9

DIRECTIONS: In each of the following tests in this part, select the letter of the one MISSPELLED word in each of the following groups of words. *PRINT THE LETTER OF THE CORRECT ANSWER IN THE SPACE AT THE RIGHT.*

1. A. statute   B. stationary   C. staturesque   D. stature   1.____
2. A. practicible   B. practical   C. particle   D. reticule   2.____
3. A. plague   B. plaque   C. ague   D. aigrete   3.____
4. A. theology   B. idealogy   C. psychology   D. philology   4.____
5. A. dilema   B. stamina   C. feminine   D. strychnine   5.____
6. A. deceit   B. benefit   C. grieve   D. hienous   6.____
7. A. commensurable   B. measurable   C. duteable   D. salable   7.____
8. A. homogeneous   B. heterogeneous   C. advantageous   D. religeous   8.____
9. A. criticize   B. dramatise   C. exorcise   D. exercise   9.____
10. A. ridiculous   B. comparable   C. merciful   D. cotten   10.____
11. A. antebiotic   B. stitches   C. pitiful   D. sneaky   11.____
12. A. amendment   B. candadate   C. accountable   D. recommendation   12.____
13. A. avocado   B. recruit   C. tripping   D. probally   13.____
14. A. calendar   B. desirable   C. familar   D. vacuum   14.____
15. A. deteriorate   B. elligible   C. liable   D. missile   15.____
16. A. amateur   B. competent   C. mischeivous   D. occasion   16.____
17. A. friendliness   B. saleries   C. cruelty   D. ammunition   17.____
18. A. wholesome   B. cieling   C. stupidity   D. eligible   18.____
19. A. comptroller   B. traveled   C. accede   D. procede   19.____
20. A. Britain   B. Brittainica   C. conductor   D. vendor   20.____

KEY (CORRECT ANSWERS)

1. C. statuesque
2. A. practicable
3. D. aigrette
4. B. ideology
5. A. dilemma

6. D. heinous
7. C. dutiable
8. D. religious
9. B. dramatize
10. D. cotton

11. A. antibiotic
12. B. candidate
13. D. probably
14. C. familiar
15. B. eligible

16. C. mischievous
17. B. salaries
18. B. ceiling
19. D. proceed
20. B. Brittanica

TEST 10

DIRECTIONS: In each of the following tests in this part, select the letter of the one MISSPELLED word in each of the following groups of words. *PRINT THE LETTER OF THE CORRECT ANSWER IN THE SPACE AT THE RIGHT.*

1. A. lengthen   B. region   C. gases   D. inspecter   1.____
2. A. imediately   B. forbidden   2.____
   C. complimentary   D. aeronautics
3. A. continuous   B. paralel   C. opposite   D. definite   3.____
4. A. Antarctic   B. Wednesday   C. Febuary   D. Hungary   4.____
5. A. transmission   B. exposure   C. pistol   D. customery   5.____
6. A. juvinile   B. martyr   C. deceive   D. collaborate   6.____
7. A. unnecessary   B. repetitive   C. cancellation   D. airey   7.____
8. A. transit   B. availible   C. objection   D. galaxy   8.____
9. A. ineffective   B. believeable   C. arrangement   D. aggravate   9.____
10. A. possession   B. progress   C. reception   D. predjudice   10.____
11. A. congradulate   B. percolate   C. major   D. leisure   11.____
12. A. convenience   B. privilige   C. emerge   D. immerse   12.____
13. A. erasable   B. inflammable   C. audable   D. laudable   13.____
14. A. final   B. fines   C. finis   D. Finish   14.____
15. A. emitted   B. representative   15.____
    C. discipline   D. insistance
16. A. diphthong   B. rarified   C. library   D. recommend   16.____
17. A. compel   B. belligerent   C. successful   D. sergeant   17.____
18. A. dispatch   B. dispise   C. dispose   D. dispute   18.____
19. A. administrator   B. adviser   C. diner   D. celluler   19.____
20. A. ignite   B. ignision   C. igneous   D. ignited   20.____

KEY (CORRECT ANSWERS)

1. D. inspector
2. A. immediately
3. B. parallel
4. C. February
5. D. customary

6. A. juvenile
7. D. airy
8. B. available
9. B. believable
10. D. prejudice

11. A. congratulate
12. B. privilege
13. C. audible
14. D. Finnish
15. D. insistence

16. B. rarefied
17. D. sergeant
18. B. despise
19. D. cellular
20. B. ignition

TEST 11

DIRECTIONS: In each of the following tests in this part, select the letter of the one MISSPELLED word in each of the following groups of words. *PRINT THE LETTER OF THE CORRECT ANSWER IN THE SPACE AT THE RIGHT.*

1. A. repellent B. secession C. sebaceous D. saxaphone 1.____

2. A. navel B. counteresolution 2.____
   C. marginalia D. perceptible

3. A. Hammerskjold B. Nehru C. U Thamt D. Krushchev 3.____

4. A. perculate B. periwinkle C. perigee D. retrogression 4.____

5. A. buccaneer B. tobacco C. buffalo D. oscilate 5.____

6. A. siege B. wierd C. seize D. cemetery 6.____

7. A. equaled B. bigoted C. benefited D. kaleideoscope 7.____

8. A. blamable B. bullrush C. questionnaire D. irascible 8.____

9. A. tobogganed B. acquiline C. capillary D. cretonne 9.____

10. A. daguerrotype B. elegiacal C. iridescent D. inchoate 10.____

11. A. bayonet B. braggadocio C. corollary D. connoiseur 11.____

12. A. equinoctial B. fusillade C. fricassee D. potpouri 12.____

13. A. octameter B. impressario C. hyetology D. hieroglyphics 13.____

14. A. innanity B. idyllic C. fylfot D. inimical 14.____

15. A. liquefy B. rarefy C. putrify D. sapphire 15.____

16. A. canonical B. stupified C. millennium D. memorabilia 16.____

17. A. paraphenalia B. odyssey 17.____
    C. onomatopoeia D. osseous

18. A. peregrinate B. pecadillo C. reptilian D. uxorious 18.____

19. A. pharisaical B. vicissitude C. puissance D. wainright 19.____

20. A. holocaust B. tesselate C. scintilla D. staccato 20.____

KEY (CORRECT ANSWERS)

1. D. saxophone
2. B. counterresolution
3. C. U Thant
4. A. percolate
5. D. oscillate

6. B. weird
7. D. kaleidoscope
8. B. bulrush
9. B. aquiline
10. A. daguerreotype

11. D. connoisseur
12. D. potpourri
13. B. impresario
14. A. inanity
15. C. putrefy

16. B. stupefied
17. A. paraphernalia
18. B. peccadillo
19. D. wainwright
20. B. tessellate

TEST 12

DIRECTIONS: In each of the following tests in this part, select the letter of the one MISSPELLED word in each of the following groups of words. *PRINT THE LETTER OF THE CORRECT ANSWER IN THE SPACE AT THE RIGHT.*

1. A. questionnaire B. gondoleer C. chandelier D. acquiescence 1.____
2. A. surveilance B. surfeit C. vaccinate D. belligerent 2.____
3. A. occassionally B. recurrence C. silhouette D. incessant 3.____
4. A. transferral B. benefical C. descendant D. dependent 4.____
5. A. separately B. flouresence C. deterrent D. parallel 5.____
6. A. acquittal B. enforceable C. counterfeit D. indispensible 6.____
7. A. susceptible B. accelarate C. exhilarate D. accommodation 7.____
8. A. impedimenta B. collateral C. liason D. epistolary 8.____
9. A. inveigle B. panegyric C. reservoir D. manuver 9.____
10. A. synopsis B. paraphernalia C. affidavit D. subpoena 10.____
11. A. grosgrain B. vermilion C. abbatoir D. connoiseur 11.____
12. A. gabardine B. camoflage C. hemorrhage D. contraband 12.____
13. A. opprobrious B. defalcate C. fiduciery D. recommendations 13.____
14. A. nebulous B. necessitate C. impricate D. discrepancy 14.____
15. A. discrete B. condescension C. condign D. condiment 15.____
16. A. cavalier B. effigy C. legitimatly D. misalliance 16.____
17. A. rheumatism B. vaporous C. cannister D. hallucinations 17.____
18. A. paleonthology B. octogenarian C. gradient D. impingement 18.____
19. A. fusilade B. fusilage C. ensilage D. desiccate 19.____
20. A. rationale B. raspberry C. reprobate D. varigated 20.____

KEY (CORRECT ANSWERS)

1. B. gondolier
2. A. surveillance
3. A. occasionally
4. B. beneficial
5. B. fluorescence

6. D. indispensable
7. B. accelerate
8. C. liaison
9. D. maneuver
10. B. paraphernalia

11. D. connoisseur
12. B. camouflage
13. C. fiduciary
14. C. imprecate
15. B. condescension

16. C. legitimately
17. C. canister
18. A. paleontology
19. A. fusillade
20. D. variegated

SPELLING

EXAMINATION SECTION

TEST 1

DIRECTIONS: Each question or incomplete statement is followed by several suggested answers or completions. Select the one that BEST answers the question or completes the statement. *PRINT THE LETTER OF THE CORRECT ANSWER IN THE SPACE AT THE RIGHT.*

Questions 1-5.

DIRECTIONS: Questions 1 through 5 consist of four words. Indicate the letter of the word that is CORRECTLY spelled.

1. A. harassment B. harrasment 1._____
   C. harasment D. harrassment

2. A. maintainance B. maintenence 2._____
   C. maintainence D. maintenance

3. A. comparable B. comprable 3._____
   C. comparible D. commparable

4. A. suficient B. sufficiant 4._____
   C. sufficient D. suficiant

5. A. fairly B. fairley C. farely D. fairlie 5._____

Questions 6-10.

DIRECTIONS: Questions 6 through 10 consist of four words. Indicate the letter of the word that is INCORRECTLY spelled.

6. A. pallor B. ballid C. ballet D. pallid 6._____

7. A. urbane B. surburbane 7._____
   C. interurban D. urban

8. A. facial B. physical C. fiscle D. muscle 8._____

9. A. interceed B. benefited 9._____
   C. analogous D. altogether

10. A. seizure B. irrelevant 10._____
    C. inordinate D. dissapproved

KEY (CORRECT ANSWERS)

1.	A	6.	B
2.	D	7.	B
3.	A	8.	C
4.	C	9.	A
5.	A	10.	D

TEST 2

DIRECTIONS: Each of Questions 1 through 15 consists of two words preceded by the letters A and B. In each question, one of the words may be spelled INCORRECTLY or both words may be spelled CORRECTLY. If one of the words in a question is spelled INCORRECTLY, print in the space at the right the capital letter preceding the INCORRECTLY spelled word. If both words are spelled CORRECTLY, print the letter C.

1. A. easely   B. readily   1.____
2. A. pursue   B. decend   2.____
3. A. measure   B. laboratory   3.____
4. A. exausted   B. traffic   4.____
5. A. discussion   B. unpleasant   5.____
6. A. campaign   B. murmer   6.____
7. A. guarantee   B. sanatary   7.____
8. A. communication B. safty   8.____
9. A. numerus   B. celebration   9.____
10. A. nourish   B. begining   10.____
11. A. courious   B. witness   11.____
12. A. undoubtedly   B. thoroughly   12.____
13. A. accessible   B. artifical   13.____
14. A. feild   B. arranged   14.____
15. A. admittence   B. hastily   15.____

KEY (CORRECT ANSWERS)

1.	A	6.	B	11.	A
2.	B	7.	B	12.	C
3.	C	8.	B	13.	B
4.	A	9.	A	14.	A
5.	C	10.	B	15.	A

TEST 3

DIRECTIONS: In each of the following sentences, one word is misspelled. Following each sentence is a list of four words taken from the sentence. Indicate the letter of the word which is MISSPELLED in the sentence. *PRINT THE LETTER OF THE CORRECT ANSWER IN THE SPACE AT THE RIGHT.*

1. The placing of any inflammable substance in any building, or the placing of any device or contrivance capable of producing fire, for the purpose of causing a fire is an attempt to burn.
    A. inflammable
    B. substance
    C. device
    D. contrivence

2. The word *break* also means obtaining an entrance into a building by any artifice used for that purpose, or by collussion with any person therein.
    A. obtaining
    B. entrance
    C. artifice
    D. colussion

3. Any person who with intent to provoke a breech of the peace causes a disturbance or is offensive to others may be deemed to have committed disorderly conduct.
    A. breech
    B. disturbance
    C. offensive
    D. committed

4. When the offender inflicts a grevious harm upon the person from whose possession, or in whose presence, property is taken, he is guilty of robbery.
    A. offender
    B. grevious
    C. possession
    D. presence

5. A person who wilfuly encourages or advises another person in attempting to take the latter's life is guilty of a felony.
    A. wilfuly
    B. encourages
    C. advises
    D. attempting

6. He maliciously demurred to an ajournment of the proceedings.
    A. maliciously
    B. demurred
    C. ajournment
    D. proceedings

7. His innocence at that time is irrelevant in view of his more recent villianous demeanor.
    A. innocence
    B. irrelevant
    C. villianous
    D. demeanor

8. The mischievous boys aggrevated the annoyance of their neighbor.
    A. mischievous
    B. aggrevated
    C. annoyance
    D. neighbor

9. While his perseverence was commendable, his judgment was debatable. 9._____
   A. perseverence B. commendable
   C. judgment D. debatable

10. He was hoping the appeal would facilitate his aquittal. 10._____
    A. hoping B. appeal
    C. facilitate D. aquittal

11. It would be preferable for them to persue separate courses. 11._____
    A. preferable B. persue
    C. separate D. courses

12. The litigant was complimented on his persistance and achievement. 12._____
    A. litigant B. complimented
    C. persistance D. achievement

13. Ocassionally there are discrepancies in the descriptions of miscellaneous items. 13._____
    A. ocassionally B. discrepancies
    C. descriptions D. miscellaneous

14. The councilmanic seargent-at-arms enforced the prohibition. 14._____
    A. councilmanic B. seargeant-at-arms
    C. enforced D. prohibition

15. The teacher had an ingenious device for maintaining attendance. 15._____
    A. ingenious B. device
    C. maintaining D. attendance

16. A worrysome situation has developed as a result of the assessment that absenteeism is increasing despite our conscientious efforts. 16._____
    A. worrysome B. assessment
    C. absenteeism D. conscientious

17. I concurred with the credit manager that it was practicable to charge purchases on a biennial basis, and the company agreed to adhear to this policy. 17._____
    A. concurred B. practicable
    C. biennial D. adhear

18. The pastor was chagrined and embarassed by the irreverent conduct of one of his parishioners. 18._____
    A. chagrined B. embarassed
    C. irreverent D. parishioners

19. His inate seriousness was belied by his flippant demeanor. 19._____
    A. inate B. belied
    C. flippant D. demeanor

20. It was exceedingly regrettable that the excessive number of challenges in the court delayed the start of the trial. 20.____
    A. exceedingly
    B. regrettable
    C. excessive
    D. challanges

KEY (CORRECT ANSWERS)

1.	D	11.	B
2.	D	12.	C
3.	A	13.	A
4.	B	14.	B
5.	A	15.	C
6.	C	16.	A
7.	C	17.	D
8.	B	18.	B
9.	A	19.	A
10.	D	20.	D

TEST 4

Questions 1-11.

DIRECTIONS: Each question consists of three words in each question, one of the words may be spelled incorrectly or all three may be spelled correctly. For each question if one of the words is spelled INCORRECTLY, write the letter of the incorrect word in the space at the right. If all three words are spelled CORRECTLY, write the letter D in the space at the right.

SAMPLE I: (A) guide   (B) departmint   (C) stranger
SAMPLE II: (A) comply   (B) valuable   (C) window
In Sample I, departmint is incorrect. It should be spelled department.
Therefore, B is the answer.
In Sample II, all three words are spelled correctly. Therefore, D is the answer.

1. A. argument   B. reciept   C. complain   1.____
2. A. sufficient   B. postpone   C. visible   2.____
3. A. expirience   B. dissatisly   C. alternate   3.____
4. A. occurred   B. noticable   C. appendix   4.____
5. A. anxious   B. guarantee   C. calendar   5.____
6. A. sincerely   B. affectionately C. truly   6.____
7. A. excellant   B. verify   C. important   7.____
8. A. error   B. quality   C. enviroment   8.____
9. A. exercise   B. advance   C. pressure   9.____
10. A. citizen   B. expence   C. memory   10.____
11. A. flexable   B. focus   C. forward   11.____

Questions 12-15.

DIRECTIONS: Each of Questions 12 through 15 consists of a group of four words. Examine each group carefully; then in the space at the right, indicate
  A. if only one word in the group is spelled correctly
  B. if two words in the group are spelled correctly
  C. if three words in the group are spelled correctly
  D. if all four words in the group are spelled correctly

12. Wendsday, particular, similar, hunderd   12.____

109

2 (#4)

13. realize, judgment, opportunities, consistent 13.____

14. equel, principle, assistense, committee 14.____

15. simultaneous, privilege, advise, ocassionaly 15.____

KEY (CORRECT ANSWERS)

1.	B	6.	D	11.	A
2.	D	7.	A	12.	B
3.	A	8.	C	13.	D
4.	B	9.	D	14.	A
5.	C	10.	B	15.	C

TEST 5

DIRECTIONS: Each of Questions 1 through 15 consists of two words preceded by the letters A and B. In each item, one of the words may be spelled INCORRECTLY or both words may be spelled CORRECTLY. If one of the words in a question is spelled INCORRECTLY, print in the space at the right the letter preceding the INCORRECTLY spelled word. If bot words are spelled CORRECTLY, print the letter C.

1. A. justified B. offering 1.____
2. A. predjudice B. license 2.____
3. A. label B. pamphlet 3.____
4. A. bulletin B. physical 4.____
5. A. assure B. exceed 5.____
6. A. advantagous B. evident 6.____
7. A. benefit B. occured 7.____
8. A. acquire B. graditude 8.____
9. A. amenable B. boundry 9.____
10. A. deceive B. voluntary 10.____
11. A. imunity B. conciliate 11.____
12. A. acknoledge B. presume 12.____
13. A. substitute B. prespiration 13.____
14. A. reputable B. announce 14.____
15. A. luncheon B. wretched 15.____

KEY (CORRECT ANSWERS)

1.	C	6.	A	11.	A
2.	A	7.	B	12.	A
3.	C	8.	B	13.	B
4.	C	9.	B	14.	A
5.	C	10.	C	15.	C

TEST 6

DIRECTIONS: Questions 1 through 15 contain lists of words, one of which is misspelled. Indicate the MISSPELLED word in each group. *PRINT THE LETTER OF THE CORRECT ANSWER IN THE SPACE AT THE RIGHT.*

1. A. felony   B. lacerate   1.____
   C. cancellation   D. seperate

2. A. batallion   B. beneficial   2.____
   C. miscellaneous   D. secretary

3. A. camouflage   B. changeable   3.____
   C. embarrass   D. inoculate

4. A. beneficial   B. disasterous   4.____
   C. incredible   D. miniature

5. A. auxilliary   B. hypocrisy   5.____
   C. phlegm   D. vengeance

6. A. aisle   B. cemetary   6.____
   C. courtesy   D. extraordinary

7. A. crystallize   B. innoculate   7.____
   C. eminent   D. symmetrical

8. A. judgment   B. maintainance   8.____
   C. bouillon   D. eery

9. A. isosceles   B. ukulele   9.____
   C. mayonaise   D. iridescent

10. A. remembrance   B. occurence   10.____
    C. correspondence   D. countenance

11. A. corpuscles   B. mischievous   11.____
    C. batchelor   D. bulletin

12. A. terrace   B. banister   12.____
    C. concrete   D. masonery

13. A. balluster   B. gutter   13.____
    C. latch   D. bridging

14. A. personnell   B. navel   14.____
    C. therefor   D. emigrant

15. A. committee B. submiting
    C. amendment D. electorate   15._____

KEY (CORRECT ANSWERS)

1.	D	6.	B	11.	C
2.	A	7.	B	12.	D
3.	C	8.	B	13.	A
4.	B	9.	C	14.	A
5.	A	10.	B	15.	B

TEST 7

Questions 1-5.

DIRECTIONS: Questions 1 through 5 consist of groups of four words. Select answer
A if only one word is spelled correctly in a group
B if TWO words are spelled correctly in a group
C if THREE words are spelled correctly in a group
D if all FOUR words are spelled correctly in a group.

1. counterfeit,   embarass,   panicky,   supercede   1.____

2. benefited,   personnel,   questionnaire,   unparalelled   2.____

3. bankruptcy,   describable,   proceed,   vacuum   3.____

4. handicapped,   mispell,   offerred,   pilgrimmage   4.____

5. corduroy,   interfere,   privilege,   separator   5.____

Questions 6-10.

DIRECTIONS: Questions 6 through 10 consist of four pairs of words each. Some of the words are spelled correctly; others are spelled incorrectly. For each question, indicate in the space at the right the letter preceding that pair of words in which BOTH words are spelled CORRECTLY.

6. A. hygienic, inviegle   B. omniscience, pittance   6.____
   C. plagarize, nullify   D. seargent, perilous

7. A. auxilary, existence   B. pronounciation, accordance   7.____
   C. ignominy, indegence   D. suable, baccalaureate

8. A. discreet, inaudible   B. hypocrisy, currupt   8.____
   C. liquidate, maintainance   D. transparancy, onerous

9. A. facility; stimulent   B. frugel, sanitary   9.____
   C. monetary, prefatory   D. punctileous, credentials

10. A. bankruptsy, perceptible   B. disuade, resilient   10.____
    C. exhilerate, expectancy   D. panegyric, disparate

Questions 11-15.

DIRECTIONS: Each question or incomplete statement is followed by several suggested answers or completions. Select the one that BEST answers the question or completes the statement. PRINT THE LETTER OF THE CORRECT ANSWER IN THE SPACE AT THE RIGHT.

11. The silent *e* must be retained when the suffix *–able* is added to the word   11._____
    A. argue   B. love   C. move   D. notice

12. The CORRECTLY spelled word in the choices below is   12._____
    A. kindergarden   B. zylophone
    C. hemorrhage   D. mayonaise

13. Of the following words, the one spelled CORRECTLY is   13._____
    A. begger   B. cemetary
    C. embarassed   D. coyote

14.
    A. dandilion   B. wiry   C. sieze   D. rythmic   14._____

15.   A. beligerent   B. anihilation
    C. facetious   D. adversery

KEY (CORRECT ANSWERS)

1.	B	6.	B	11.	D
2.	C	7.	D	12.	C
3.	D	8.	A	13.	D
4.	A	9.	C	14.	B
5.	D	10.	D	15.	C

TEST 8

DIRECTIONS: In each of the following sentences, one word is misspelled. Following each sentence is a list of four words taken from the sentence. Indicate the letter of the word which is MISSPELLED. *PRINT THE LETTER OF THE CORRECT ANSWER IN THE SPACE AT THE RIGHT.*

1. If the administrator attempts to withold information, there is a good likelihood that there will be serious repercussions.
   A. administrator
   B. withold
   C. likelihood
   D. repercussions

   1.____

2. He condescended to apologize, but we felt that a beligerent person should not occupy an influential position.
   A. condescended
   B. apologize
   C. beligerent
   D. influential

   2.____

3. Despite the sporadic delinquent payments of his indebtedness, Mr. Johnson has been an exemplery customer.
   A. sporadic
   B. delinquent
   C. indebtedness
   D. exemplery

   3.____

4. He was appreciative of the support he consistantly acquired, but he felt that he had waited an inordinate length of time for it.
   A. appreciative
   B. consistantly
   C. acquired
   D. inordinate

   4.____

5. Undeniably they benefited from the establishment of a receivership, but the question of statutary limitations remained unresolved.
   A. undeniably
   B. benefited
   C. receivership
   D. statutary

   5.____

6. Mr. Smith profered his hand as an indication that he considered it a viable contract, but Mr. Nelson alluded to the fact that his colleagues had not been consulted.
   A. profered
   B. viable
   C. alluded
   D. colleagues

   6.____

7. The treatments were beneficial according to the optomotrists, and the consensus was that minimal improvement could be expected.
   A. beneficial
   B. optomotrists
   C. consensus
   D. minimal

   7.____

8. Her frivolous manner was unbecoming because the air of solemnity at the cemetery was pervasive.
   A. frivalous
   B. solemnity
   C. cemetery
   D. pervasive

   8.____

9. The clandestine meetings were designed to make the two adversaries more amicable, but they served only to intensify their emnity.
   A. clandestine   B. adversaries
   C. amicable   D. emnity

   9._____

10. Do you think that his innovative ideas and financial acumen will help stabalize the fluctuations of the stock market?
    A. innovative   B. acumen
    C. stabalize   D. fluctuations

    10._____

11. In order to keep a perpetual inventory, you will have to keep an uninterrupted surveillance of all the miscellanious stock.
    A. perpetual   B. uninterrupted
    C. surveillance   D. miscellanious

    11._____

12. She used the art of pursuasion on the children because she found that caustic remarks had no perceptible effect on their behavior.
    A. pursuasion   B. caustic
    C. perceptible D. effect

    12._____

13. His sacreligious outbursts offended his constituents, and he was summarily removed from office by the City Council.
    A. sacreligious   B. constituents
    C. summarily   D. Council

    13._____

14. They exhorted the contestants to greater efforts, but the exhorbitant costs in terms of energy expended resulted in a feeling of lethargy.
    A. exhorted   B. contestants
    C. exhorbitant D. lethargy

    14._____

15. Since he was knowledgable about illicit drugs, he was served with a subpoena to appear for the prosecution.
    A. knowledgable   B. illicit
    C. subpoena   D. prosecution

    15._____

16. In spite of his lucid statements, they denigrated his report and decided it should be succintly paraphrased.
    A. lucid   B. denigrated
    C. succintly D. paraphrased

    16._____

17. The discussion was not germane to the contraversy, but the indicted man's insistence on further talk was allowed.
    A. germane   B. contraversy
    C. indicted D. insistence

    17._____

18. The legislators were enervated by the distances they had traveled during the election year to fullfil their speaking engagements.
    A. legislators   B. enervated
    C. traveled   D. fullfil

    18._____

19. The plaintiffs' attornies charge the defendant in the case with felonious assault.   19._____
    A. plaintiffs'   B. attornies
    C. defendant   D. felonious

20. It is symptomatic of the times that we try to placate all, but a proposal for new forms of disciplinery action was promulgated by the staff.   20._____
    A. symptomatic   B. placate
    C. disciplinery   D. promulgated

KEY (CORRECT ANSWERS)

1.	B	11.	D
2.	C	12.	A
3.	D	13.	A
4.	B	14.	C
5.	D	15.	A
6.	A	16.	C
7.	B	17.	B
8.	A	18.	D
9.	D	19.	B
10.	C	20.	C

TEST 9

DIRECTIONS: Each of Questions 1 through 15 consists of a single word which is spelled either correctly or incorrectly. If the word is spelled CORRECTLY, you are to print the letter C (Correct) in the space at the right. If the word is spelled INCORRECTL, you are to print the letter W (Wrong).

1. pospone   1._____
2. diffrent   2._____
3. height   3._____
4. carefully   4._____
5. ability   5._____
6. temper   6._____
7. deslike   7._____
8. seldem   8._____
9. alcohol   9._____
10. expense   10._____
11. vegatable   11._____
12. dispensary   12._____
13. specemin   13._____
14. allowance   14._____
15. exersise   15._____

KEY (CORRECT ANSWERS)

1. W	6. C	11. W
2. W	7. W	12. C
3. C	8. W	13. W
4. C	9. C	14. C
5. C	10. C	15. W

TEST 10

DIRECTIONS: Each of Questions 1 through 10 consists of four words, one of which may be spelled incorrectly or all four words may be spelled correctly. If one of the words in a question is spelled incorrectly, print in the space at the right the capital letter preceding the word which is spelled INCORRECTLY. If all four words are spelled CORRECTLY, print the letter E.

1. A. dismissal   B. collateral   1.____
   C. leisure   D. proffession

2. A. subsidary   B. outrageous   2.____
   C. liaison   D. assessed

3. A. already   B. changeable   3.____
   C. mischevous   D. cylinder

4. A. supersede   B. deceit   4.____
   C. dissension   D. imminent

5. A. arguing   B. contagious   5.____
   C. comparitive   D. accessible

6. A. indelible   B. existance   6.____
   C. presumptuous   D. mileage

7. A. extention   B. aggregate   7.____
   C. sustenance   D. gratuitous

8. A. interrogate   B. exaggeration   8.____
   C. vacillate   D. moreover

9. A. parallel   B. derogatory   9.____
   C. admissible   D. appellate

10. A. safety   B. cumalative   10.____
    C. disappear   D. usable

KEY (CORRECT ANSWERS)

1.	D	6.	B
2.	A	7.	A
3.	C	8.	E
4.	E	9.	C
5.	C	10.	B

TEST 11

DIRECTIONS: Each of questions 1 through 10 consists of four words, one of which may be spelled incorrectly or all four words may be spelled correctly. If one of the words in a question is spelled INCORRECTLY, print in the space at the right the capital letter preceding the word which is spelled incorrectly. If all four words are spelled CORRECTLY, print the letter E.

1. A. vehicular   B. gesticulate   1.____
   C. manageable D. fullfil

2. A. inovation   B. onerous   2.____
   C. chastise   D. irresistible

3. A. familiarize B. dissolution   3.____
   C. oscillate   D. superflous

4. A. census   B. defender   4.____
   C. adherence   D. inconceivable

5. A. voluminous   B. liberalize   5.____
   C. bankrupcy   D. conversion

6. A. justifiable B. executor   6.____
   C. perpatrate D. dispelled

7. A. boycott   B. abeyence   7.____
   C. enterprise D. circular

8. A. spontaineous B. dubious   8.____
   C. analyze   D. premonition

9. A. intelligible B. apparently   9.____
   C. genuine   D. crucial

10. A. plentiful   B. ascertain   10.____
    C. carreer   D. preliminary

KEY (CORRECT ANSWERS)

1. D   6. C
2. A   7. B
3. D   8. A
4. E   9. E
5. C   10. C

TEST 12

DIRECTIONS: Each of questions 1 through 25 consists of four words, one of which may be spelled incorrectly or all four words may be spelled correctly. If one of the words in a question is spelled INCORRECTLY, print in the space at the right the capital letter preceding the word which is spelled incorrectly. If all four words are spelled CORRECTLY, print the letter E.

1. A. temporary   B. existance   1.____
   C. complimentary   D. altogether

2. A. privilege   B. changeable   2.____
   C. jeopardize   D. commitment

3. A. grievous   B. alloted   3.____
   C. outrageous   D. mortgage

4. A. tempermental   B. accommodating   4.____
   C. bookkeeping   D. panicky

5. A. auxiliary   B. indispensable   5.____
   C. ecstasy   D. fiery

6. A. dissappear   B. buoyant   6.____
   C. imminent   D. parallel

7. A. loosly   B. medicine   7.____
   C. schedule   D. defendant

8. A. endeavor   B. persuade   8.____
   C. retroactive   D. desparate

9. A. usage   B. servicable   9.____
   C. disadvantageous   D. remittance

10. A. beneficary   B. receipt   10.____
    C. excitable   D. implement

11. A. accompanying   B. intangible   11.____
    C. offerred   D. movable

12. A. controlling   B. seize   12.____
    C. repetitious   D. miscellaneous

13. A. installation   B. accommodation   13.____
    C. consistant   D. illuminate

14. A. incidentaly   B. privilege   14.____
    C. apparent   D. chargeable

122

2 (#12)

15. A. prevalent   B. serial   15.____
    C. briefly   D. disatisfied

16. A. reciprocal   B. concurrence   16.____
    C. persistence D. withold

17. A. deferred   B. suing   17.____
    C. fulfilled D. pursuant

18. A. questionable   B. omission   18.____
    C. acknowledgment D. insistent

19. A. guarantee   B. committment   19.____
    C. mitigate   D. publicly

20. A. prerogative   B. apprise   20.____
    C. extrordinary D. continual

21. A. arrogant   B. handicapped   21.____
    C. judicious D. perennial

22. A. permissable   B. deceive   22.____
    C. innumerable   D. retrieve

23. A. notable   B. allegiance   23.____
    C. reimburse D. illegal

24. A. wholly   B. disbursement   24.____
    C. hindrance D. conciliatory

25. A. guidance   B. condemn   25.____
    C. publically D. coercion

KEY (CORRECT ANSWERS)

1. B
2. E
3. B
4. A
5. E

6. A
7. A
8. D
9. B
10. A

11. C
12. E
13. C
14. A
15. D

16. D
17. E
18. A
19. B
20. C

21. E
22. A
23. E
24. E
25. C

SPELLING
EXAMINATION SECTION
TEST 1

DIRECTIONS: In each of the following groups of words, only one of the words is misspelled. In each group, select the misspelled word and then write the letter of your choice in the answer space at the right.

1. A. cafeteria B. patron C. amateur 1.____
    D. perceive E. pledgeing

2. A. requirement B. financial C. accesory 2.____
    D. government E. college

3. A. approxamate B. mirror C. destroy 3.____
    D. disregard E. promising

4. A. sincerely B. discern C. wrangle 4.____
    D. truly   E. audiovisual

5. A. tomatoes B. purity C. negligent 5.____
    D. dramatize E. plentiful!

6. A. theoretical B. seige C. C. volcano 6.____
    D. innocence E. dexterity

7. A. tommorrow B. reluctant C. shady 7.____
    D. unveil   E. lightning

8. A. auction B. lenient C. prejudice 8.____
    D. sculpter E. originally

9. A. rhapsody B. perplex C. obtuse 9.____
    D. mortgage E. quandery

10. A. friendless B. hundreth C. singular 10.____
    D. channel   E. attitude

11. A. missile B. propelled C. beautefy 11.____
    D. spirited E. spectacles

12. A. spaghetti B. missionery C. twelfth 12.____
    D. vegetable E. stifle

13. A. corrode B. hygiene C. irrelevant 13.____
    D. asociate E. maintenance

14. A. monogram B. minister C. criticle 14.____
    D. frequency E. genuine

15. A. introduce B. thematic C. economy 15.____
    D. valuable E. laborer

16. A. precede B. defalt C. heathen 16.____
    D. attain E. conscious

17. A. greivance B. chivalry C. scary 17.____

2 (#1)

    D. obscure   E. pastime

18. A. assurance   B. immoderate   C. patriotism   18.____
    D. combustible   E. stressfull

19. A. inginuity   B. legitimate   C. schedule   19.____
    D. accompanying   E. substantial

20. A. grafics   B. merger   C. global   20.____
    D. sensitive   E. exhibit

KEY (CORRECT ANSWERS)

	CORRECT SPELLING			CORRECT SPELLING
1.	E, pledging	11.	C,	beautify
2.	C, accessory	12.	B,	missionary
3.	A, approximate	13.	D,	associate
4.	D, truly	14.	C,	critical
5.	E, plentiful	15.	E,	laborer
6.	B, siege	16.	B,	default
7.	A, tomorrow	17.	A,	grievance
8.	D, sculptor	18.	E,	stressful
9.	E, quandary	19.	A,	ingenuity
10.	B, hundredth	20.	A,	graphics

TEST 2

DIRECTIONS: In each of the following groups of words, only one of the words is misspelled. In each group, select the misspelled word and then write the letter of your choice in the answer space at the right.

1. A. pierce B. irritible C. ceiling 1._____
   D. portfolio E. hereditary

2. A. meanness B. anxious C. challange 2._____
   D. grief E. priority

3. A. anouncement B. politeness C. routine 3._____
   D. dependable E. bashful

4. A. scold B. pigeon C. transistor 4._____
   D. stomach E. decietful

5. A. antibiotic B. exagerate C. anticipation 5._____
   D. heavily E. essential

6. A. embarrass B. friendly C. diameter 6._____
   D. quite E. anguler

7. A. suffix B. persuade C. morgage 7._____
   D. exclusive E. pertinent

8. A. prologue B. gaseous C. stallion 8._____
   D. indevisible E. erroneous

9. A. acquarium B. tireless C. starred 9._____
   D. fried E. erroneous

10. A. innocent B. automatic C. reign 10._____
    D. primative E. substitute

11. A. satisfactory B. deceived C. existence 11._____
    D. anceint E. resolving

12. A. scandalize B. conferred C. aptitude 12._____
    D. spirited E. assurred

13. A. convenient B. already C. savage 13._____
    D. acheivement E. schedule

14. A. intercede B. cashier C. leisurely 14._____
    D. barameter E. interrelated

15. A. brittle B. freight C. rigidity 15._____
    D. tobacco E. excellance

16. A. ballet B. biscuit C. whimsecal 16._____
    D. inertia E. endeavor

17. A. intentionally B. mysterious C. nickel 17._____
    D. indicisive E. guarantee

18.	A. occurred	B. calendar	C. sophmore	18.___
	D. extension	E. prevail		
19.	A. truant	B. syllabus	C. justifyable	19.___
	D. peasant	E. library		
20.	A. recomendation	B. unanimous	C. symmetrical	20.___
	D. manageable	E. necessity		

KEY (CORRECT ANSWERS)

	CORRECT SPELLING			CORRECT SPELLING
1.	B, irritable		11.	D, ancient
2.	C, challenge		12.	E, assured
3.	A, announcement		13.	D, achievement
4.	E, deceitful		14.	D, barometer
5.	B, exaggerate		15.	E, excellence
6.	E, angular		16.	C, whimsical
7.	C, mortgage		17.	D, indecisive
8.	D, indivisible		18.	C, sophomore
9.	A, aquarium		19.	C, justifiable
10.	D, primitive		20.	A, recommendation

TEST 3

DIRECTIONS: In each of the following groups of words, only one of the words is misspelled. In each group, select the misspelled word and then write the letter of your choice in the answer space at the right.

1. A. artillery   B. patriotism   C. fiery   1.____
   D. avalanche   E. lieing

2. A. glossery   B. omitted   C. noticeable   2.____
   D. gaseous   E. loveless

3. A. convocation B. particularly C. prevailing   3.____
   D. recollect   E. impressonable

4. A. incompetent B. heredity   C. medicinal   4.____
   D. sustained   E. turmoil

5. A. forgetting   B. argument   C. apparantly   5.____
   D. secrecy   E. monopoly

6. A. against   B. furthermore   C. brief   6.____
   D. explore   E. unanamous

7. A. suspision   B. formerly   C. opportunity   7.____
   D. concentrate E. intelligent

8. A. league   B. analyze   C. bribery   8.____
   D. usully   E. straighten

9. A. rediculous   B. recommend   C. vengeance   9.____
   D. cemetery   E. library

10. A. mountain   B. percentage   C. manageable   10.____
    D. unisen   E. truly

11. A. caffeine   B. tecnique   C. invisible   11.____
    D. possession E. relieve

12. A. referral   B. debtor   C. shineing   12.____
    D. acceptable E. laborer

13. A. apology   B. reputation   C. sensible   13.____
    D. infansy   E. eloquent

14. A. angrily   B. umbrella   C. observent   14.____
    D. fiend   E. inquiry

15. A. earnest   B. transfered   C. responsible   15.____
    D. drunkenness E. portable

16. A. almanac   B. entangle   C. managing   16.____
    D. persistant E. indulge

17. A. exploit   B. jewelry   C. siege   17.____
    D. summary   E. tomato

129

18.	A. occur	B. villain	C. disastrous	18.____
	D. entirely	E. calculater		
19.	A. hurrying	B. immense	C. aggressive	19.____
	D. victim	E. exclusivly		
20.	A. businesslike	B. miracle	C. equipment	20.____
	D. explanatory	E. division		

KEY (CORRECT ANSWERS)

CORRECT SPELLING

1. E, lying
2. A, glossary
3. E, impressionable
4. B, hereditary
5. C, apparently
6. E, unanimous
7. A, suspicion
8. D, usually
9. A, ridiculous
10. D, unison

CORRECT SPELLING

11. B, technique
12. C, shining
13. D, infancy
14. C, observant
15. B, transferred
16. D, persistent
17. B, jewelry
18. E, calculator
19. E, exclusively
20. D, explanatory

TEST 4

DIRECTIONS: In each of the following groups of words, only one of the words is misspelled. In each group, select the misspelled word and then write the letter of your choice in the answer space at the right.

1. A. rapture   B. fictitious   C. inocence   1.____
   D. humorous   E. cyclical

2. A. abnormality B. fidelity   C. hybrid   2.____
   D. harpoon   E. antaganist

3. A. actually   B. interupt   C. inspiration   3.____
   D. equipped   E. squirrel

4. A. hypothisis B. popularity   C. hypnosis   4.____
   D. acceptable E. convertible

5. A. inconveniance B. humidity   C. ninety   5.____
   D. radiant   E. campaign

6. A. caucus   B. secede   C. gallent   6.____
   D. erroneous E. crisis

7. A. interaction B. coalition   C. philosophy   7.____
   D. guarantee E. treachary

8. A. prairie   B. propeller   C. strategy   8.____
   D. divisible E. secretery

9. A. merchant   B. obsticle   C. parcel   9.____
   D. altitude   E. ignorant

10. A. choral   B. acommodate   C. capacity   10.____
    D. neighborly E. deodorant

11. A. arrangement B. gradually   C. portable   11.____
    D. aristacrat E. junction

12. A. umbrella   B. grandeur   C. familar   12.____
    D. infinite   E. calorie

13. A. purgatory B. inprisonment C. hopeless   13.____
    D. division   E. awkward

14. A. fascinate B. disimilar   C. luscious   14.____
    D. immaculate E. persuasive

15. A. traffic   B. senseless   C. rhythm   15.____
    D. acclaim   E. grammar

16. A. stagnation B. ambivalence   C. twelfth   16.____
    D. territory E. adherance

17. A. desireable B. physics   C. predominant   17.____
    D. malaria   E. corrupt

18.	A. nuisance D. development	B. hysteria E. ratify	C. equivalent	18.___
19.	A. faulty D. tomorrow	B. seize E. traction	C. suspence	19.___
20.	A. reliable D. carrying	B. luxurious E. divisable	C. preoccupied	20.___

KEY (CORRECT ANSWERS)

CORRECT SPELLING

1. C, innocence
2. E, antagonist
3. B, interrupt
4. A, hypothesis
5. A, inconvenience
6. C, gallant
7. E, treachery
8. E, secretary
9. B, obstacle
10. B, accommodate

CORRECT SPELLING

11. D, aristocrat
12. C, familiar
13. B, imprisonment
14. B, dissimilar
15. D, acclaim
16. E, adherence
17. A, desirable
18. C, equivalent
19. C, suspense
20. E, divisible

TEST 5

DIRECTIONS: In each of the following groups of words, only one of the words is misspelled. In each group, select the misspelled word and then write the letter of your choice in the answer space at the right.

1. A. candidate   B. merchandise   C. soloes   1._____
   D. source   E. siphon

2. A. scent   B. sovereign   C. banana   2._____
   D. gardner   E. career

3. A. theoretical B. bagage   C. consequence   3._____
   D. bargain   E. encouraging

4. A. simultaneous B. leisure   C. twilight   4._____
   D. cloride   E. muffle

5. A. excessive   B. pennant   C. misfit   5._____
   D. vineger   E. kerosene

6. A. strength   B. medley   C. cannibal   6._____
   D. reciept   E. decency

7. A. accidentally B. shield   C. advising   7._____
   D. treasury   E. disconfort

8. A. vengeful   B. miniature   C. alliance   8._____
   D. comprehensable E. prohibited

9. A. psychiatrist B. grievance   C. barbecue   9._____
   D. formerly   E. controled

10. A. journel   B. shadowy   C. tomorrow   10._____
    D. convertible E. macaroni

11. A. despair   B. receiver   C. instance   11._____
    D. langauge   E. convertible

12. A. brevity   B. height   C. apolegy   12._____
    D. shield   E. engagement

13. A. acceptence B. arbitrary   C. hypnotism   13._____
    D. physician E. quarrel

14. A. zoology   B. armory   C. cemetery   14._____
    D. frivolous E. honorery

15. A. triple   B. tough   C. trifel   15._____
    D. tongue   E. terrible

16. A. luscious   B. adaquate   C. temporary   16._____
    D. ghostly   E. umbrella

17. A. genuine   B. hygeine   C. omission   17._____
    D. sincerely E. bracelet

133

2 (#5)

18.	A. symptom D. skeleton	B. specialty E. flammible	C. available	18.____
19.	A. spaghetti D. worthyness	B. locale E. parcel	C. practice	19.____
20.	A. testamonial D. apathetic	B. corruption E. tissue	C. aggravate	20.____

___

KEY (CORRECT ANSWERS)

		CORRECT SPELLING				CORRECT SPELLING
1.	C,	solos		11.	D,	language
2.	D,	gardener		12.	C,	apology
3.	B,	baggage		13.	A,	acceptance
4.	D,	chloride		14.	E,	honorary
5.	D,	vinegar		15.	C,	trifle
6.	D,	receipt		16.	B,	adequate
7.	E,	discomfort		17.	B,	hygiene
8.	D,	comprehensible		18.	E,	flammable
9.	E,	controlled		19.	D,	worthiness
10.	A,	journal		20.	A,	testimonial

www.ingramcontent.com/pod-product-compliance
Lightning Source LLC
Chambersburg PA
CBHW082124230426
43671CB00015B/2803